THICK AND THIN

Thick and Thin

Moral Argument at Home and Abroad

MICHAEL WALZER

University of Notre Dame Press
Notre Dame   London

Library of Congress Cataloging-in-Publication Data

Walzer, Michael.
    Thick and thin: moral argument at home and abroad /
Michael Walzer.
        p.   cm.
    Includes bibliographical references and index.
    ISBN 0-268-01884-7 (alk. paper)
    1. Distributive justice.   2. Pluralism (Social sciences)
3. Democracy.   4. Political ethics.   5. International relations—
Moral and ethical aspects.   6. Self-determination, National.
I. Title.
JC575.W35   1994   93-43201
172—dc20   CIP

for Sally H. Walzer

שַׁקַּמְתִּי אֵם בְּיִשְׂרָאֵל

Judges 5:7

Contents

Introduction

My aim in this book is twofold: first, to rehearse, revise, and extend a set of arguments about justice, social criticism, and nationalist politics that I have been involved in making for some ten years. The revisions and extensions also represent so many responses to my critics (I am grateful to all of them). But I shall not engage in any polemics here; I want only to get the arguments right—what that might mean is taken up in my third chapter—not to gain some advantage in the critical wars. These are wars that can never in any case be won, since none of the participants are inclined, nor can they be forced, to surrender. There is no final arbiter, like the sovereign in Hobbes's *Leviathan*. So I shall strengthen my arguments as best I can and wait for further criticism. Nothing in these pages is finished or done with.

But I also want, second, to put my arguments to work in the new political world that has arisen since I first presented them. This new world is marked by the collapse of the totalitarian project—and then by a pervasive, at least ostensible, commitment to democratic government and an equally pervasive, and more actual, commitment to cultural autonomy and national independence. A universal or near-universal ideology side-by-side with an extraordinarily intense pursuit of the "politics of difference": what are we to make of this? The two are not necessarily incompatible, though their simultaneous success is bound to pluralize democracy in a radical way. It will produce a number of different "roads to democracy" and a variety of "democracies" at the end of the road—a prospect difficult to accept for those who believe that democracy is the single best form of government. And sometimes, at least, difference will triumph at the expense of democracy, generating political regimes more closely attuned to this or that historical culture: religious republics, liberal oligarchies, military chiefdoms, and so on. Nonetheless, I want to endorse the politics of difference and, at the same time, to describe and defend a certain sort of universalism. This won't be a universalism that requires democratic government in all times and places, but it opens the way for democracy wherever there are enough prospective and willing citizens. More important, perhaps, it prohibits the brutal repression of both minority and majority groups in democratic and non-democratic states. (I count myself among the willing citizens; I think it best to be governed democratically; but I don't claim that my political views have the definitive endorsement of God or Nature or History or Reason.)

Difference is, as it has always been, my major theme and abiding interest. But I mean to begin, in the first chapter, by describing what I take to be a universal moment—not a philosophical but an actual moment—and the politics and morality it requires. I will then go on to restate my own particularist account of justice, in the second chapter, and of social criticism, in the third—always keeping in mind the memory of the universal moment. In the fourth chapter, I will try to show how the universalism of "self-determination," always congenial to difference, can also constrain it, setting limits to our particularist projects. And at the end, in the fifth chapter, I will provide a differentiated account of the self that will, I hope, render my defense of difference elsewhere more plausible and persuasive. When I wrote *Spheres of Justice* ten years ago, I argued (and I still believe) that we need focus only on things, the objects of distribution, to work out a critical account of distributive justice. The account does not require or "rest on" a theory of human nature. But there is a picture of the self, nothing so grand as a theory, that is consistent with "complex equality" as I described it there and with versions of complexity that I have defended elsewhere. So I will appeal, at the end, to the inner divisions of my readers—assuming that these are not unlike my own—and invite them to recognize themselves in the thick, particularist stories I want to tell about distributive justice, social criticism, and national identity.

I will describe in these chapters two different but interrelated kinds of moral argument—a way of talking among ourselves, here at home, about the thickness of our own history and culture (including our democratic political culture) and a way of talking to people abroad, across different cultures, about the thinner life we have in common. "There is a thin man inside every fat man," George Orwell once wrote, "just as . . . there's a statue inside every block of stone."[1] Similarly, there are the makings of a thin and universalist morality inside every thick and particularist morality—but the story of these two is not at all like the statue and the stone. They are differently formed and differently related, as we shall see.

---

[1] George Orwell, *Coming Up for Air* (New York: Harcourt, Brace, 1950), Part 1, chapter 3. I have borrowed the idea of thickness from Clifford Geertz's defense of "thick description" in his much-cited *The Interpretation of Cultures* (New York: Basic Books, 1973), see especially chap. 1. But it is not my claim to offer a thick description of moral argument, rather to point to a kind of argument that is itself "thick"— richly referential, culturally resonant, locked into a locally established symbolic system or network of meanings. "Thin" is simply the contrasting term; its use is illustrated in the first chapter.

ONE: *Moral Minimalism*

I

I want to begin my argument by recalling a picture (I have in mind a film clip from the television news, late in that wonderful year 1989), which is the actual starting point, the conceptual occasion, of this chapter. It is a picture of people marching in the streets of Prague; they carry signs, some of which say, simply, "Truth" and others "Justice." When I saw the picture, I knew immediately what the signs meant—and so did everyone else who saw the same picture. Not only that: I also recognized and acknowledged the values that the marchers were defending—and so did (almost) everyone else. Is there any recent account, any post-modernist account, of political language that can explain this understanding and acknowledgment? How could I penetrate so quickly and join so unreservedly in the language game or the power play of a distant demonstration? The marchers shared a culture with which I was largely unfamiliar; they were responding to an experience I had never had. And yet, I could have walked comfortably in their midst. I could carry the same signs.

The reasons for this easy friendliness and agreement probably have as much to do with what the marchers did not mean as with what they did mean. They were not marching in defense of the coherence theory, or the consensus theory, or the correspondence theory of truth. Perhaps they disagreed about such theories among themselves; more likely, they did not care about them. No particular account of truth was at issue here. The march had nothing to do with epistemology. Or, better, the

1

epistemological commitments of the marchers were so elementary that they could be expressed in any of the available
theories—except for those that denied the very possibility
of statements being "true." The marchers wanted to hear
true statements from their political leaders; they wanted
to be able to believe what they read in the newspapers;
they didn't want to be lied to anymore.

Similarly, these citizens of Prague were not marching in
defense of utilitarian equality or John Rawls's difference
principle or any philosophical theory of desert or merit or
entitlement. Nor were they moved by some historical
vision of justice with roots, say, in Hussite religious radi-
calism. Undoubtedly, they would have argued, if pressed,
for different distributive programs; they would have described a just society in different ways; they would have
urged different rationales for reward and punishment; they
would have drawn on different accounts of history and culture. What they meant by the "justice" inscribed on their
signs, however, was simple enough: an end to arbitrary ar-
rests, equal and impartial law enforcement, the abolition
of the privileges and prerogatives of the party elite—
common, garden variety justice.

II

Moral terms have minimal and maximal meanings; we
can standardly give thin and thick accounts of them, and
the two accounts are appropriate to different contexts,
serve different purposes. It's not the case, however, that
people carry around two moralities in their head, two
understandings of justice, for example, one of which is
brought out for occasions like the Prague march while the
other is held in readiness for the debates soon to be joined
on taxation or welfare policy. The march, it might be argued, is an appeal for support abroad; the debates will
draw on home truths and local values; hence the reliance

on garden variety justice in the first case and on more highly cultivated and deeply rooted varieties of justice in the second. But this is not the way the distinction works. Rather, minimalist meanings are embedded in the maximal morality, expressed in the same idiom, sharing the same (historical/cultural/religious/political) orientation. Minimalism is liberated from its embeddedness and appears independently, in varying degrees of thinness, only in the course of a personal or social crisis or a political confrontation—as, in the Czech case, with communist tyranny. Because (most of) the rest of us have some sense of what tyranny is and why it is wrong, the words used by the demonstrators shed whatever particularist meanings they may have in the Czech language; they become widely, perhaps universally accessible. Were there no common understanding of tyranny, access would fail. At the same time, the same words have further meanings for the marchers, which they will argue about among themselves and which we, looking on from far away, may well miss. They resonate differently in Prague than their translations resonate in, say, Paris or New York.

The contemporary argument about relativism and universalism is probably best understood as an argument about the extent and legitimacy of those resonances. What range of difference can the idea of morality cover? I want to suggest a way of thinking about this question that attends to the experience of the Prague marchers. Clearly, when they waved their signs, they were not relativists: they would have said, rightly, it seems to me, that everyone in the world should support their cause—should join them in defense of "truth" and "justice" (I am quoting the signs, not expressing irony or skepticism about their message). But when they turn to the business of designing a health care system or an educational system for Czechs and Slovaks or arguing about the politics of their union or separation, they will not be universalists: they will aim at what is best for themselves, what fits their history and culture, and won't insist that all the rest of us endorse or reiterate their decisions.[2]

This dualism is, I think, an internal feature of every morality. Philosophers most often describe it in terms of a (thin) set of universal principles adapted (thickly) to these or those historical circumstances. I have in the past suggested the image of a core morality differently elaborated in different cultures.[3] The idea of elaboration is better than adaptation, it seems to me, because it suggests a process less circumstantial and constrained, more freely creative: governed as much by ideal as by practical considerations. It accounts better for the actual differences that anthropology and comparative history reveal. But both these descriptions suggest mistakenly that the starting point for the development of morality is the same in every case. Men and women everywhere begin with some common idea or principle or set of ideas and principles, which they then work up in many different ways. They start thin, as it were, and thicken with age, as if in accordance with our deepest intuition about what it means to develop or mature. But our intuition is wrong here. Morality is thick from the beginning, culturally integrated, fully resonant, and it reveals itself thinly only on special occasions, when moral language is turned to specific purposes.

Consider, further, the idea of justice. It appears, so far as I can tell, in every human society—the idea itself, some word or set of words that give it a name, institutions and practices that are supposed to make it real, to exemplify

---

[2] In fact, the argument for separation is a minimalist and universal one, invoking the principle of self-determination (see Chapter Three). But whatever cooperative arrangements are worked out for the new states will obviously depend upon more particular understandings.

[3] Michael Walzer, *Interpretation and Social Criticism* (Cambridge, Mass.: Harvard University Press, 1987), pp. 23–25.

justice or to enact and enforce it. And so when we read in
the book of Deuteronomy, say, "Justice, justice, shalt thou
pursue," we have no difficulty agreeing; we fill in our own
developed understanding of justice (this is the subject of
my second chapter), which indeed guides or which we acknowledge ought to guide our political and legal pursuits.[4]
But if someone were to produce for us a thick description
of what the Deuteronomist actually meant—a close
reading of the text, a reconstruction of the historical
context—we would not find it so easy to agree. We might
well prefer a response more complex, differentiated, or
ambiguous than simple agreement. Or the description
might seem so distant and alien as to leave us entirely un-
responsive (but we will still recognize it as a description of
"justice"). Again, when the prophet Isaiah condemns as
unjust the practices he calls "grinding the face of the
poor," he escapes, at least for the moment, all complexity:
that is unjust simply.[5] We know it to be so even if we don't
know with the same certainty and unanimity what would
count as treating the poor justly. A maximalist account of
practices and institutions, which Isaiah's criticism probably presupposes, would leave many of us wondering if
justice could really require anything quite like that.

Whatever the origins of the idea of justice, whatever
the starting point of the argument in this or that society,
people thinking and talking about justice will range over
a mostly familiar terrain and will come upon similar
issues—like political tyranny or the oppression of the
poor. What they say about these issues will be part and
parcel of what they say about everything else, but some
aspect of it—its negativity perhaps, its rejection of brutal-
ity ("grinding the face")—will be immediately accessible

---

[4] Deuteronomy 16:20.
[5] Isaiah 3:15.

to people who don't know anything about the other parts
and parcels. Pretty much anybody looking on will see
something here that they recognize. The sum of these
recognitions is what I mean by minimal morality.

I want to stress (though it should already be obvious)
that "minimalism" does not describe a morality that is
substantively minor or emotionally shallow. The opposite
is more likely true: this is morality close to the bone.
There isn't much that is more important than "truth" and
"justice," minimally understood. The minimal demands
that we make on one another are, when denied, repeated
with passionate insistence. In moral discourse, thinness
and intensity go together, whereas with thickness comes
qualification, compromise, complexity, and disagreement.

III

For many philosophers (in both the Anglo-American
and continental traditions) minimal morality is little more
than an invitation to further work. Moral philosophy is
usually understood as a twofold enterprise that aims, first,
at providing a foundation for minimalism and, second, at
building on that foundation a more expansive structure. I
suppose that the goal is a singular and more or less complete account of what we ought to do and how we ought
to live, an account that can then be used as a critical standard for all the more circumstantial constructions of
particular societies and cultures. The search for singularity
is probably overdetermined in Western philosophy, but it
is more specifically inspired here by the apparent singularity of the moral minimum or, at least, by the fact of
general agreement on such minimalist values as "truth"
and "justice." If we agree this far and, it appears, so easily,
why not seek a larger even if more difficult agreement?

Some thirty years ago, a group of American painters,
who were also theorists of painting, aspired to something

they called Minimal Art.[6] The capital letters derive from some manifesto calling for a form of art that was "objective and unexpressive." I am not sure what those words mean when applied to a painting, but they nicely capture one view of minimalism in morality. Applied to a moral rule, they mean that the rule serves no particular interest, expresses no particular culture, regulates everyone's behavior in a universally advantageous or clearly correct way. The rule carries no personal or social signature. (I don't know if Minimal Art was signed.) Though it may have been taught with special force by this or that individual, it was never his or hers. Though it was first worked out in a specific time and place, it bears no mark of its origin. This is the standard philosophical view of moral minimalism: it is everyone's morality because it is no one's in particular; subjective interest and cultural expression have been avoided or cut away. And if we succeed in understanding this morality, we should be able to construct a complete objective and unexpressive code—a kind of moral Esperanto.

But this hope is misbegotten, for minimalism is neither objective nor unexpressive. It is reiteratively particularist and locally significant, intimately bound up with the maximal moralities created here and here and here, in specific times and places. Hence when we see the Prague marchers, we don't in the first instance (or perhaps ever) endorse "truth" and "justice" as abstract propositions. Rather, we recognize the occasion; we imaginatively join the march; our endorsement is more vicarious than detached and speculative. We too don't want to be told lies; we too remember, or we have listened to stories about, tyranny and

---

[6] On Minimal Art, see *The Oxford Companion to Twentieth-Century Art*, ed. Harold Osborne (Oxford: Oxford University Press, 1981), pp. 375–377.

oppression. We see the point of the Czech signs. At the same time, however, we give to "truth" and "justice" our own additional meanings; we allow them their full expressive range within our own culture. So while we march in spirit with the men and women of Prague, we have in fact our own parade. (This may seem less than obvious in the case at hand, since Prague is culturally a nearby place. Imagine, then, a march for "truth" and "justice" in Rangoon or Beijing.)

We march vicariously with people in trouble whoever they are; and we have our own parade. This dualist metaphor captures our moral reality. We should not try to escape the dualism, for it fits what I am inclined to call the necessary character of any human society: universal because it is human, particular because it is a society. Philosophers commonly try, as I have already suggested, to make the adjective dominant over the noun, but the effort cannot be sustained in any particular society except at a cost (in coercion and uniformity) that human beings everywhere will recognize as too high to pay. That recognition vindicates at once minimalism and maximalism, the thin and the thick, universal and relativist morality. It suggests a general understanding of the value of living in a particular place, namely, one's own place, one's home or homeland. Societies are necessarily particular because they have members and memories, members *with* memories not only of their own but also of their common life. Humanity, by contrast, has members but no memory, and so it has no history and no culture, no customary practices, no familiar life-ways, no festivals, no shared understanding of social goods. It is human to have such things, but there is no singular human way of having them. At the same time, the members of all the different societies, because they are human, can acknowledge each other's different ways, respond to each other's cries for help, learn from each other, and march (sometimes) in each other's parades.

Why isn't this enough? Think of the exodus of Israel from Egypt, the *Anabasis*, Muhammad's *hegira*, the Pilgrims' crossing of the Atlantic, the Boer trek, the long march of the Chinese communists, the Prague demonstrations: must all these merge into one grand parade? There is nothing to gain from the merger, for the chief value of all this marching lies in the particular experience of the marchers. They can join each other only for a time; there is no reason to think that they are all heading in the same direction. The claim that they must be heading in the same direction, since there is only one direction in which good-hearted (or ideologically correct) men and women can possibly march, is an example—so writes the Czech novelist Milan Kundera in *The Unbearable Lightness of Being*—of leftist *kitsch*.[7] It is also an example of philosophical highmindedness. But it does not fit our moral experience.

IV

It is possible, nonetheless, to give some substantial account of the moral minimum. I see nothing wrong with the effort to do that so long as we understand that it is necessarily expressive of our own thick morality. A moral equivalent of Esperanto is probably impossible—or, rather, just as Esperanto is much closer to European languages than to any others, so minimalism when it is expressed as Minimal Morality will be forced into the idiom and orientation of one of the maximal moralities. There is no neutral (unexpressive) moral language. Still, we can pick out from among our values and commitments those that make it possible for us to march vicariously with the

[7] Milan Kundera, *The Unbearable Lightness of Being* (New York: Harper and Row, 1984), Part VI: "The Grand March."

people in Prague. We can make a list of similar occasions
(at home, too) and catalogue our responses and try to figure out what the occasions and the responses have in
common. Perhaps the end product of this effort will be
a set of standards to which all societies can be held—
negative injunctions, most likely, rules against murder,
deceit, torture, oppression, and tyranny. Among ourselves,
late twentieth-century Americans or Europeans, these
standards will probably be expressed in the language of
rights, which is the language of our own moral maximalism. But that is not a bad way of talking about injuries and
wrongs that no one should have to endure, and I assume
that it is translatable.

A morality that did not allow for such talk, whose prac-
titioners could not respond to other people's pain and
oppression or march (sometimes) in other people's parades, would be a deficient morality. A society or political
regime (like that of the Czech communists) that violated
the minimal standards would be a deficient society. In this
sense, minimalism provides a critical perspective. But I
want to stress again that the moral minimum is not a free-
standing morality. It simply designates some reiterated
features of particular thick or maximal moralities. Hence
I am inclined to doubt that when we criticize other societies we are best described as applying minimal standards;
at least, that can't be all that we are doing. It is, of course,
the minimalism of "truth" and "justice" that makes it possible for us to join the Prague marchers. But when we
criticize Czech communism in ways that suggest an alternative, we move quickly beyond the minimum, knowing
that some of what we say will echo positively in Prague
(or in this or that part of Prague) and some, perhaps,
won't. Criticizing tyranny, for example, I am likely to defend the values of social democracy, though these are not
by any means the universal values of anti-tyrannical politics. Other criticisms of tyranny will repeat one part of my
argument and ignore or reject other parts. But I have no

philosophical reason to separate out the parts (I may have political or prudential reasons).

The critical enterprise is necessarily carried on in terms of one or another thick morality. The hope that minimalism, grounded and expanded, might serve the cause of a universal critique is a false hope. Minimalism makes for a certain limited, though important and heartening, solidarity. It doesn't make for a full-blooded universal doctrine. So we march for a while together, and then we return to our own parades. The idea of a moral minimum plays a part in each of these moments, not only in the first. It explains how it is that we come together; it warrants our separation. By its very thinness, it justifies us in returning to the thickness that is our own. The morality in which the moral minimum is embedded, and from which it can only temporarily be abstracted, is the only full-blooded morality we can ever have. In some sense, the minimum has to be there, but once it is there, the rest is free. We ought to join the marchers in Prague, but once we have done that, we are free to argue for whatever suits our larger moral understandings. There is one march, and there are many (or, there are many marches, and then sometimes there is one).

V

I need to discuss a contemporary version of moral minimalism that claims to respect the one and the many but in fact does not. It is popular these days to think of the minimum in procedural terms—a thin morality of discourse or decision that governs every particular creation of a substantive and thick morality. Minimalism, on this view, supplies the generative rules of the different moral maximums. A small number of ideas that we share or should share with everyone in the world guides us in producing the complex cultures that we don't and needn't share—and so they explain and justify the production. Commonly, as in Jürgen Habermas's critical theory, these shared ideas require a democratic procedure—indeed, they require a radical democracy of articulate agents, men and women who argue endlessly about, say, substantive questions of justice.[8] Minimal morality consists in the rules of engagement that bind all the speakers; maximalism is the never-finished outcome of their arguments.

This ingenious doctrine faces two serious difficulties. First of all, the procedural minimum turns out to be rather more than minimal. For the rules of engagement are designed to ensure that the speakers are free and equal, to liberate them from domination, subordination, servility, fear, and deference. Otherwise, it is said, we could not respect their arguments and decisions. But once rules of this sort have been laid out, the speakers are left with few substantive issues to argue and decide about. Social structure, political arrangements, distributive standards are pretty much given; there is room only for local adjustments. The thin morality is already very thick—with an entirely decent liberal or social democratic thickness. The rules of engagement constitute in fact a way of life. How could they not? Men and women who acknowledge each other's equality, claim the rights of free speech, and practice the virtues of tolerance and mutual respect, don't leap from the philosopher's mind like Athena from the head of Zeus. They are creatures of history; they have been worked on, so to speak, for many generations; and they inhabit a society that "fits" their qualities and so supports, reinforces,

---

[8] Jürgen Habermas, *Moral Consciousness and Communicative Action*, trans. Christian Lenhardt and Shierry Weber Nicholsen (Cambridge, Mass.: MIT Press, 1990); Seyla Benhabib, *Critique, Norm, and Utopia: A Study of the Foundations of Critical Theory* (New York: Columbia University Press, 1986), chapter 8.

and reproduces people very much like themselves. They are maximalists even before they begin their rule-governed discussions.

The second difficulty perhaps only restates the first. Rules of engagement assume, obviously, that in the beginning there are rules and then there are engagements. Minimalism precedes maximalism; once we were thin but have grown thick. I have already disputed this view; now with the example of discourse and decision theory before us we can more easily understand its problems. For the minimal morality prescribed by these theories is simply abstracted from, and not very far from, contemporary democratic culture. If no such culture existed, this particular version of minimal morality would not even be plausible to us. Maximalism in fact precedes minimalism. But no particular maximum is the sole source of the moral minimum, let alone of all the other maximums. When full-grown democrats imagine that the rules of discursive engagement are the generative rules of morality in all its kinds, they are very much like an oak tree that, endowed with speech and encouraged to speak freely, solemnly declares the acorn to be the seed and source of the entire forest.

But this at least suggests a certain generosity. What is perhaps a better analogue would be provided by an oak tree that acknowledged the full range of arboreal difference and then argued for the cutting down of all those trees, now called illegitimate, that did not begin as acorns. So (some) proceduralist philosophers argue for the rejection of any morality that is not or could not be produced by their procedure.[9] Moral minimalism has indeed a critical function. If, however, every maximum but one (our own) is ruled out,

---

[9] I think that this is the argument of Bruce Ackerman's *Social Justice in the Liberal State* (New Haven, Conn.: Yale University Press, 1980).

we can immediately adopt that one as our critical standard: why bother with minimalism at all? Unless we can identity a neutral starting point from which many different and possibly legitimate moral cultures might develop, we can't construct a proceduralist minimum. But there is no such starting point. Moralities don't have a common beginning; the men and women who work them out are not like runners in a race—who also have a common set of rules and a common goal, neither of which play a part in the less organized work of cultural elaboration.

A far more modest proceduralism has recently been urged by Stuart Hampshire (in his book *Innocence and Experience*), who defends what he calls "a thin notion of minimum procedural justice . . . the conditions of mere decency."[10] Hampshire is inclined to identify these conditions with the common (he says "species-wide") experience of political deliberation. He aims to derive from this experience a set of practical rules or understandings that might protect men and women from cruelty and oppression. His is clearly an argument for "truth" and "justice"—always in a minimalist style: just enough of the two so that the larger argument about truth and justice can go on and on. The larger argument has no necessary form; many different forms (not only democratic ones) meet the requirements of mere decency. Hampshire is not in the business of inventing or deducing ideal procedures to govern the argument and give shape and legitimacy to its outcomes. Outcomes can be right or wrong, good or bad, in a more local and particularist sense. What is important is that they be reached without tyrannical coercion or civil war. I take this to be a useful way of getting at the substance of moral minimalism; it is also, and this may be more important, a way closely attuned to twentieth-

---

[10] Stuart Hampshire, *Innocence and Experience* (Cambridge, Mass.: Harvard University Press, 1989), esp. pp. 72–78.

century political experience. I would insist, however, that it isn't the only way.

Proceduralism is appealing because it ostensibly (in Hampshire's case, actually) allows for divergent outcomes; it locates commonality on the way to difference. We might also, however, reverse the argument, acknowledge the great diversity of historical processes, and look for similar or overlapping outcomes: locate commonality at the end-point of difference. Often, certainly, we put together the moral minimum by abstracting from social practices re-iterated in many countries and cultures (rather than from the process of reiteration). The practice of government, for example, brings with it ideas about the responsibility of governors toward the governed. The practice of war brings with it ideas about combat between combatants, the exclu-sion of non-combatants, civilian immunity. The practice of commerce brings with it ideas about honesty, fair-dealing, and fraud. All these ideas are ineffective much of the time, no doubt, or they work only within highly elabo-rated cultural systems that give to each constituent practice a radically distinct form. Nonetheless, the ideas are avail-able for minimalist use when occasions arise to use them.

VI

Now let's consider one possible occasion very much in today's news: when the solidarity we feel with people in trouble, confronting murder and oppression, seems to require not only marching but also fighting—military inter-vention on their behalf. No doubt, we should never be in a hurry to fight; I have argued elsewhere for a strong pre-sumption against intervening in other people's countries.[11] Nor can every moral rule that we are able to describe in

---

[11] *Just and Unjust Wars* (New York: Basic Books, 1977), chapter 6.

minimalist terms serve to justify the use of force. We are
more likely called upon to speak up for "truth" than to fight
for it. "Justice," too, is better defended with the moral support of outsiders than with their coercive intervention. We
might even say that this preference is a feature of the moral
minimum. Nonetheless, there are times when it is morally
justified to send armed men and women across a border—
and minimalism alone (ultra-minimalism?) defines the time
and fixes its limits.

So we intervene, if not on behalf of "truth" and "justice," then on behalf of "life" and "liberty" (against
massacre or enslavement, say). We assume that the people
we are trying to help really want to be helped. There may
still be reasons for holding back, but the belief that these
people prefer to be massacred or enslaved won't be among
them. Yes, some things that we consider oppressive are
not so regarded everywhere. The consideration is a feature
of our own maximal morality, and it cannot provide us
with an occasion for military intervention. We cannot
conscript people to march in our parade. But minimalism
makes for (some) presumptive occasions, in politics just as
it does in private life. We will use force, for example, to
stop a person from committing suicide, without knowing
in advance who he is or where he comes from. Perhaps he
has reasons for suicide confirmed by his maximal morality,
endorsed by his moral community. Even so, "life" is a reiterated value and defending it is an act of solidarity. And
if we give up the forcible defense out of respect for his
reasons, we might still criticize the moral culture that provides those reasons: it is insufficiently attentive, we might
say, to the value of life.

VII

Minimal morality is very important, both for the sake
of criticism and for the sake of solidarity. But it can't sub-

stitute for or replace the defense of thickly conceived values. Social democracy, market freedom, moral laissez-faire, republican virtue, this or that idea of public decency or the good life—all these have to be defended in their own terms. Our arguments on their behalf are likely to be inclusive of the moral minimum, but they are not continuous with it, not derived from it or entailed by it. If we are to make these arguments properly, honestly, we have to be clear about their status: they are *ours*, not, until we have persuaded the others, everyone's. Minimalism, by contrast, is less the product of persuasion than of mutual recognition among the protagonists of different fully developed moral cultures. It consists in principles and rules that are reiterated in different times and places, and that are seen to be similar even though they are expressed in different idioms and reflect different histories and different versions of the world. I won't consider here the reasons for the reiterations or for the differences (a naturalistic account seems best for the first, a cultural account for the second). It is enough to stress the dual effect of these principles and rules. In context, everyday, they provide contrasting perspectives; seen from a distance, in moments of crisis and confrontation, they make for commonality.

I should stress that what is recognized is just this (partial) commonality, not the full moral significance of the other cultures. Most people most of the time do not see the others, in context, as carriers of value; most people are not pluralists. Cultural pluralism is a maximalist idea, the product of a thickly developed liberal politics. Minimalism depends on something less: most simply, perhaps, on the fact that we have moral expectations about the behavior not only of our fellows but of strangers too. And they have overlapping expectations about their own behavior and ours as well. Though we have different histories, we have common experiences and, sometimes, common responses, and out of these we fashion, as needed, the moral minimum. It is a jerry-built and ramshackle affair—as hastily put together as the signs for the Prague march.

Minimalism, then, is quite unlike Orwell's statue, liberated from the shapeless stone. We have in fact no knowledge of the stone; we begin with the finished statue; maximalist in style, ancient, carved by many hands. And then, in moments of crisis, we hastily construct an abstract version, a stick figure, a cartoon, that only alludes to the complexity of the original. We seize upon a single aspect, relevant to our immediate (often polemical) purposes and widely recognizable. What unites us at such a time is more the sense of a common enemy than the commitment to a common culture. We don't all possess or admire the same statue, but we understand the abstraction. It is the product of a historical conjuncture, not of a philosophical "in-the-beginning."

Minimalism is not foundational: it is not the case that different groups of people discover that they are all committed to the same set of ultimate values. Among the supporters of the Prague demonstrations, to take an easy example, were Christian fundamentalists for whom secular "truth" and "justice" are not the most important things. But they too can join in celebrating the downfall of the regime of lies. Often enough, what goes deepest for one group (personal salvation or the knowledge of God, say) is likely to mean little to another—so that the first group is hard pressed to understand how members of the second can possibly be moral men and women. We are constantly surprised by goodness in others, like the rabbis of ancient Israel by "righteous gentiles" or Jesuit missionaries by the godless Chinese or cold war Americans by communist dissidents. We share some values with these others, including important values, for which it is sometimes necessary to march (and sometimes to fight). But the minimum is not the foundation of the maximum, only a piece of it. The value of minimalism lies in the encounters it facilitates, of which it is also the product. But these encounters are not—not now, at least—sufficiently sustained to produce a thick morality. Minimalism leaves room for thickness elsewhere; indeed, it presupposes thickness elsewhere. If we did not have our own parade, we could not march vicariously in Prague. We would have no understanding at all of "truth" or "justice."

TWO: *Distributive Justice As A Maximalist Morality*

I

I want to take distributive justice as an example of a thick or maximalist morality. No doubt there are minimalist versions; I will say something about them later on. But any full account of how social goods ought to be distributed will display the features of moral maximalism: it will be idiomatic in its language, particularist in its cultural reference, and circumstantial in the two senses of that word: historically dependent and factually detailed. Its principles and procedures will have been worked out over a long period of time through complex social interactions. Arguments among individuals and groups are an important part of these interactions; they don't, however, constitute the set, which also includes social conflict, political bargaining, cultural imitation, and (sometimes) religious revelation. The process as a whole is virtually impossible to reconstruct, but it is surely misrepresented when it is described, late in the day, as if it had been guided from the beginning by a single, comprehensive, and universal principle. All such principles are abstractions and simplifications that, when analyzed, reveal their idiomatic, particularist, and circumstantial character.

Consider the ancient Greek maxim according to which we ought "to give every man his due." This maxim epitomizes, first, a profoundly hierarchical (and, no doubt, sexist) understanding of both the social and moral worlds and then a fairly complacent conviction that the two worlds are cognitively accessible in detail. There was no single measure of "dueness" among the Greeks (though social status and moral virtue tended to run together), but one knew, nonetheless, what was due to oneself and to everyone else. The signs were assumed to be evident or at least available, and they were also assumed to differentiate individuals in a conventionally graded way, from higher to lower, more to less worthy.[12] Though the maxim is reproduced in Justinian's *Code*, it is pre-Christian and non-Christian in its origin and meaning. Hamlet's famous question

> Use every man after his desert,
> and who would 'scape whipping?

reflects a very different world view.[13] I doubt that the Greeks ever imagined the radical egalitarianism of universal depravity, which would indeed turn their maxim into a frightening distributive principle. In its time and place, however, it doesn't seem to have been at all frightening; its advocates, for all their recognition of the world's uncertainties, were sure enough, most of the time, that they would be well served if they were given their due, used after their deserts.

A similar analysis can be made of the maxim that epitomizes (though with less claim to completeness) liberal or bourgeois justice: equality of opportunity or, in the more evocative style of the French Revolution, "the career open to talents." It might be said that nothing more is being

---

[12] Cf. Aristotle's more complicated formulation: "Justice is relative to persons; and a just distribution is one in which the relative values of the things given correspond to those of the persons receiving . . ." *Politics*, 1280a (trans. Ernest Barker [Oxford: Oxford University Press, 1948], p. 136). For the simpler version, see K. J. Dover, *Greek Popular Morality in the Time of Plato and Aristotle* (Berkeley: University of California Press, 1974), pp. 180–183.

[13] *Institutes* I.i.1; *Hamlet* II.ii.

claimed here than the superiority of one kind of "dueness" over another: virtue or talent must override or, better, must determine social status. Indeed, these are the slogans of the long struggle against hereditary privilege. But they reflect also a wholly new understanding of everyday life. Careers are to be *open*, that is, free from the obstacles of a stratified system—but also deprived of any sort of guarantee. Talents are not simply recognized and rewarded; they must be deployed in a free competition for whatever opportunities are available. There is no necessary match of talents and opportunities, let alone of talents and rewards. What is (morally) necessary is only an equality of chances, which is also an equality of risk. Hierarchy is replaced by universal striving and contention, romantically celebrated as the seed-bed of individuality and self-realization.

This self that struggles to realize itself is well known to us; it is the subject of most Western and modern theories of distributive justice. We are likely to think of it in the first person singular—as John Rawls, for example, invites us to do when we put ourselves, each one of us, in the original position and ask what social arrangements would best suit our (possible or conceivable) life plans.[14] It is not every kind of life that is lived according to a plan. Today we commonly think of our lives as projects, undertakings in which we ourselves are the undertakers, the entrepreneurs, the managers and organizers of our own activities. And the set of our activities, extended over time, planned in advance, aimed at a goal (a respected place in the social system or a conventionally recognized accomplishment)—this is what we mean by a *career*. The word first appears in English with this meaning in 1803; it obviously comes earlier in French, but probably not very much earlier.

---

[14] On life plans, see Rawls, *A Theory of Justice* (Cambridge, Mass.: Harvard University Press, 1971), pp. 407–416.

But this is a historically specific and peculiar under-standing of a human life. Think of the alternatives: (1) an inherited life, where I simply take over the place and accomplishments of my parents and make them my own; (2) a socially regulated life, where I get precisely what is due to my birth or my virtue; (3) a spontaneous life, ran-domly constituted by circumstance and impulse; (4) a divinely ordained or predestined life, where the plan is God's, not mine, and I obey his will insofar as I can make it out. "Equality of opportunity" is a possible, and a valu-able, distributive principle only when significant numbers of men and women have given up these alternatives and come to think of their lives as careers. For it is the oppor-tunity to pursue that kind of life that is now being distributed. Or, more directly, if we think of the full range of distributive procedures sanctioned by the maxim—admission and appointment committees, anti-nepotism and anti-discrimination laws, civil service exams, and so on—careers themselves are being distributed. But this can only be done if there are people with ambitions of the appropriate kind, who intend to have a career.

So we are distributing lives of a certain sort, and what counts as justice in distribution depends on what that "sort" is or, better, on the meaning of lives like that for the people whose lives they are. We also distribute life itself, mere life, physical life, which is given and taken in courts of law judging capital cases, or on the battlefield, or in hos-pitals. Here the criteria are entirely different; we make no inquiry into the talent or the professional qualifications of the defendant, the enemy soldier, or the patient. It is the guilt or innocence of the defendant, the threat posed by the enemy, and the illness of the patient that determine our responses. Of course, talent and qualification are not the only criteria ruled out in these distributions of life and death but also social status, wealth, and political power: I will come back to exclusions of this latter sort later on.

Cases of triage are different again. Now we are likely to sort people out according to their life chances. We will not treat the most sick or the most severely injured first (nor, presumably, the wealthiest or the most famous), but attend instead to those who have the greatest chance to seize their chances: life is given to those who might still pursue a lifelong career. I suppose that this is what equality of opportunity requires under conditions of crisis. In times and places where human life was differently understood, different criteria applied. Consider, for example, the medieval Jewish laws that regulated the ransoming of captives, an unhappily frequent necessity that was assigned first place in the distributive hierarchy, first call on communal resources. But what to do when there were many captives and resources were short? The rules of triage required that women be ransomed before men, scholars before laymen.[15] Women came first because their honor (or purity) as well as their lives were at risk in captivity; scholars came first because their lives were of greater value to the community (they were also the authors of the legal texts in which this value was assigned). I can imagine a number of ways to criticize each of these priorities, but we must first understand them. The idea of life as a chosen career, valued because of the choice, is wholly alien to the people who worked them out. And if it was also alien to the people whose lives were at stake, then *this* critical principle, equality of opportunity, individual autonomy, is probably not one that we can usefully or rightly apply to the medieval case.

---

[15] Maimonides, "Gifts to the Poor" 8:10–18 in *The Code of Maimonides*, VII: *The Book of Agriculture*, trans. Isaac Klein (New Haven: Yale University Press, 1979), pp. 82–84.

II

I came to the basic idea of *Spheres of Justice* by reflecting on examples like these, in which the governing principles did not seem to have the universal reach that philosophers commonly look for. The basic idea is that distributive justice must stand in some relation to the goods that are being distributed. And since these goods have no essential nature, this means that it must stand in some relation to the place that these goods hold in the (mental and material) lives of the people among whom they are distributed. Hence my own maxim: distributive justice is relative to social meanings.[16] I now hasten to add, given the storm of criticism this maxim has provoked, *not relative simply*, for justice in distributions is a maximalist morality, and it takes shape along with, constrained by, a reiterated minimalism—the very idea of "justice," which provides a critical perspective and a negative doctrine. Murder as a way of distributing life and death, for example, whether it is the work of a neighborhood thug or the secret police, is everywhere ruled out. The rule will be expressed in different cultural idioms, but its meaning, and even its reasons, will be more readily available to outsiders than will the meaning of human life as a career, an inheritance, or a divine gift. And our solidarity with people threatened by murderers is easier, quicker, and more obvious than with people struggling against religious prophets, or aristocratic families, or bourgeois careerists.

There is another constraint built into my "relativist" maxim: the reference to social meanings requires some understanding of how such meanings are constituted and how they can be recognized. I suppose that they must meet

---

[16] Michael Walzer, *Spheres of Justice: A Defense of Pluralism and Equality* (New York: Basic Books, 1983), chapter 1.

certain criteria—non-substantive but not merely formal. They must actually be shared across a society, among a group of people with a common life; and the sharing cannot be the result of radical coercion. Since all socialization is coercive, this is again a minimalist principle. It doesn't require that social meanings be worked out or agreed to in anything like the Habermasian ideal speech situation. All that it requires is that the extorted agreement of slaves to their slavery, to take another easy example, should not count in establishing the common understandings of a society.[17] We must look for real agreements of the sort illustrated by the contemporary view of life-as-a-career. We reach such a view at the end of a complex historical process, and in that process coercion undoubtedly has a part—think of the French (and every other) Revolution— but not such a part as to render the agreement spurious, a mere trick of the powerful.

Social meanings are not just *there*, agreed on once and for all. Meanings change over time as a result of internal tension and external example; hence, they are always subject to dispute. The fact that there actually are disputes, radically different interpretations of social meaning, fierce intellectual and political battles over this or that social good, has led critics to question the relativity of distributions to meanings. If meanings are disputed and therefore, in the absence of a supreme judge, indeterminate, what is the nature of the relation? Well, what is it that's in dispute? What do we argue about? Someone insists, say, that in cases of triage we should attend only to life chances: his interpretation of life-as-a-career is singular and absolute. Someone else argues that we should attend also to

---

[17] The moral relation of slaves and masters is probably better understood by thinking about just and unjust wars than about distributive justice: see *Spheres of Justice*, p. 250n.

suffering: her interpretation is more qualified. They may indeed disagree fiercely, but they are arguing within a world they share, where the range of social meanings is fairly narrow. Medieval Jews would have difficulty joining the argument, even if they could (as I think they could) figure it out. And, very often, distributive disputes take an even narrower form than this: we find ourselves in agreement on the meaning of the disputed good and even on the principle of allocation that follows from that meaning, and we argue only about the application of the principle in these or those circumstances. Indeed, agreements on the most critical social goods are commonly both deep and long lasting, so that we are likely to recognize them and understand how they change over time and how they come into dispute only if we turn away from more immediate and local arguments and take the long view. We will never grasp the idea of social meaning unless we get its horizons right.

III

Consider, then, the cure of souls and the cure of bodies in the medieval and modern West—my favorite example from *Spheres of Justice* and one that I would like, someday, to develop at length.[18] The most striking feature of the medieval cure of souls is its socialized character. The Christian world was organized so as to make repentance and salvation universally available. The availability was financed with public funds (tithes) and regulated by ecclesiastical laws that provided for the presence of a priest in every parish, the catechism of children, confession and communion at fixed intervals. This elaborate distributive machinery is best understood, it seems to me, as a function

---

[18] *Spheres of Justice*, p. 87.

of the social meaning of the good that was being distributed: eternal life. I can't attempt here to describe what this good actually meant in the common life of medieval Christians. The everyday role of eternity is no doubt a difficult matter, especially for those of us who have lost or given up its comforts. It is enough to say that eternity was both real and important or, more precisely, that medieval Christians agreed on its reality and importance. And from this agreement there followed the moral necessity of socialized distribution.[19]

The cure of bodies, by contrast, was commonly taken to be less real or less certain and also less important, and so it was left in private hands. No one seems to have worried much about the fact that wealthy and powerful men and women had access to medical treatment unavailable to anyone else. Church officials who tolerated a similar distribution of pastoral care were more likely to be the objects of critical attack. The priestly "pluralist" who collected tithes from several parishes and served none of them, living in the capital city and attending the powerful, is a common figure of medieval and early modern satire. Courtly physicians, who were also paid out of public funds, were not thought to have the same sort of socially extended obligations.

None of this seems unjust to me—and this is not because I am bound by my "relativist" maxim to defer to the conventions of the age (any age). For if these conventions were imposed by force, the mere ideology of the ruling class, the idea of social meaning might usefully be deployed in criticism of them. But what we have here is a maximalist morality, a thick understanding of life and death, a human culture. To this we ought certainly to defer, for it

---

[19] Marshall W. Baldwin, *The Medieval Church* (Ithaca: Cornell University Press, 1953), introduction and chapter 1.

makes no moral sense to wag our finger at medieval Christians, insisting that they *should have had* our understanding of life and death. But we can criticize the distributions they enforced insofar as we think of these as options for ourselves. I doubt, in fact, that most of us could do anything but criticize them, so considered, for we are the products of a profound cultural transformation.

Over a long period of time, ordinary men and women came increasingly to question the reality or the central importance or the public availability of eternal life. We might say that they substituted longevity for eternity—though I am sure that longevity was always considered a good thing. It is not so much that it became a better thing, but rather that the advance of medical knowledge made it more available and so more highly valued. Descartes, who was in this case a prophet as much as a philosopher, anticipated the advance and its effects when he wrote in his *Discourse on Method* that "the preservation of health" was "no doubt the chief of all goods." He proposed to spend the rest of his life in pursuit of medical knowledge so "that we might be liberated from a number of disorders, both of mind and body, and perhaps also from the feebleness of old age"—as convinced of the possibility of success as medieval Christians had been when they pursued the knowledge of God and the liberation of the spirit.[20]

The increasing recognition of health and longevity as goods of great value and ready availability brought with it an increasing public commitment, first to the prevention of disease and then to individual therapy. The cure of bodies was gradually socialized, even as the cure of souls was being privatized. Tax money was assigned to public health, hospital construction, medical training, and much else,

---

[20] René Descartes, *Discourse on Method*, trans. Arthur Wollaston (Hammondsworth: Penguin Classics, 1960), p. 85.

and the state's coercive powers were enlisted (to require vaccination, for example). But eternal life ceased to be recognized as a social good in which the public and its agencies might legitimately take an interest.

It seems to me impossible to look at this long process of cultural transformation and pick out the precise moment at which justice required socialized health care or ceased to require socialized salvation. One can imagine an extended period of time during which a strong case might have been made for public support of both the cure of souls and the cure of bodies, or of either one, or, perhaps, of neither one. What is striking, however, is that no case can be made today, in the West, for the use of the state's coercive power to require religious communion or church attendance; and despite the continuing debate over health care in this country, I am inclined to say that no case can be made today for the disengagement of the state from the cure of bodies. What forms socialized care should take, exactly how egalitarian it ought to be, what scope should be allowed to the private practice of medicine, how coercive the state can be (in the case of medical testing, say, or of safety laws): all this is still subject to debate, much as the extent and legitimacy of coercion in religious matters—forced attendance at church services, for example—was debated in the early modern period. But the gross structure of justice-in-cures is given in advance of these arguments.

The arguments are necessarily local in character, precisely because they follow from or build upon deep cultural understandings. No one in Prague, say, will be moved to demonstrate on behalf of American advocates of national health insurance; that campaign is an example of what I mean by "our own parade." Nor, needless to say, would taxation for medical services or even the restraint of private enterprise in health care provide a legitimate occasion for military intervention in our affairs (in the name of "liberty").

IV

So: we cannot decide on the distribution of medical and pastoral care until we understand the meaning of longevity and eternity in the lives of the people who are being cared for. We must *attend to the goods*—not to the good (in the singular) because even if Descartes was right when he called health the "chief" good, it is not the only one; nor does the quality that gives it its "chiefness" determine the relative value of all the other goods. They are independently valued in accordance with the place they hold in the lives of their valuers. Nor do I believe, despite Descartes's assignment of primacy, that there is any *summum bonum* or overall hierarchy of goods. When conflicts arise, we will argue about priorities, offering different interpretations of the place of this or that good in our common life. But conflicts don't always arise. Social meanings and the principles and processes they entail are commonly distinct and autonomous. Indeed, autonomy is a basic distributive principle, itself entailed by the differentiation of goods. When we distribute careers (or career opportunities) to the talented, or health care to the sick, or salvation to the faithful, we are rejecting the claims of the well-born, the well-off, and the powerful. Each social good has a separate set of legitimate claimants. And so we might well go on to recognize the claims of the well-born to social status, say, or the well-off to market commodities, or the powerful to political influence.

Each of these latter claims requires, of course, extended discussion and qualification; I don't mean to endorse them in any simple way. But they are claims of the right sort, which is to say, differentiated and specific. If we insist on differentiation and specificity across the range of claims, the sum of our rejections, recognitions, and qualifications will yield what I want to call "complex equality," a social condition where no group of claimants dominates the different distributive processes. No one good rules over all the others, such that possessing it brings everything else in train. Justice requires the defense of difference—different goods distributed for different reasons among different groups of people—and it is this requirement that makes justice a thick or maximalist moral idea, reflecting the actual thickness of particular cultures and societies.

Simple and straightforward equality is a very thin idea, reiterated in one form or another in (almost) every distributive system, and useful in the criticism of certain gross injustices, but quite incapable of governing the full range of distributions. It serves more as a constraint, a kind of critical minimalism—as when we say that someone is not being treated "like a human being" or when we condemn racial discrimination. Any effort to enforce equality across the board is immediately self-contradictory, for the enforcement would require a radical concentration, and therefore a radically unequal distribution, of political power. A simple and straightforward hierarchy—the old over the young, the educated over the ignorant, the well-born over the low-born—makes even more directly for domination; it is simply the triumph of one good over all the others. Each of the goods that have shaped conventional hierarchies can play its part in a complex distributive system: seniority in the management of a factory or company, for example, learning in the organization of a school or academy, familial reputation in the social register and the gossip column. But a society in which any one of these was effectively dominant would be a one-dimensional, a frighteningly thin, society.

Though the twentieth century provides some striking examples of the perverse utopianism of simple equality, the major challenge to distributive justice—in the past and in our own time—comes from the effort to deploy a single good across the range of goods. I have used the spatial imagery of "spheres" to describe this deployment. Think of each social good as enclosed within boundaries fixed by the reach of its entailed distributive principles and the legitimate authority of its distributive agents. Then the deployment of one good outside its sphere—money is the obvious example—is a kind of illegitimate boundary crossing, an act of distributive aggression. When such acts are occasional, they are likely to be seen as cases of corruption or, more evocatively, as scandals. A wealthy man is caught trying to bribe a public official: he is crossing illegitimately from the sphere of the market, where money counts, to the political sphere, where it is not supposed to count. Caught in the act, he will be condemned by the press and perhaps also by the courts—for in the effort to stop such boundary crossings we have made bribery illegal. But if the wealthy as a class have public officials in their pocket, as it were, if the crossing has already been effected and the corruption has become systematic, then what we have is not scandal but tyranny. We usually recognize tyranny by boundary crossings the other way, as in the classic definition of the tyrant as a political ruler who seizes the daughters and the money of his subjects, deploying his power in the domestic and market spheres.[21] But any aggression makes for tyranny; plutocrats are tyrants too, even if their rule has non-political origins. Indeed, this is the standard form of tyranny in capitalist societies.

If we attend to the goods that are being distributed, and to their social meaning, and to the principles and procedures that follow from their meaning, then we will be able to recognize scandalous and tyrannical boundary crossings. These are not the only forms of injustice, but they are the most common forms in any society that has achieved some significant degree of differentiation. The theory of complex equality provides an account of what is wrong with plutocracy, theocracy, meritocracy, geron-

---

[21] See Machiavelli's advice to his prince to avoid injustice of this sort, if only for prudential reasons: *The Prince*, chapter 17.

tocracy, technocracy, and every other effort to make one good, and the qualities associated with its possession, dominant over all other goods and qualities. This is the critical force of the theory. I want to stress that this criticism, directed against aggressive boundary crossings, is also a *defense of boundaries*. An alternative criticism of established systems of distributive justice aims to abolish the boundaries and the differences among spheres—in the belief that society is (really) all of a piece. Its protagonists hold that theories of social differentiation and complex equality are in fact ideologies, disguising the actual unity of society and then, depending on the direction from which this criticism comes, either dividing the opponents of the ruling class or fostering an illegitimate opposition. Consider now two versions of this alternative view.

On the left, or some parts of the left, society is said to be wholly political, such that all decisions, in personal and domestic life, in the market, in churches, hospitals, and friendly associations, and of course in the state, reflect a unified pattern of domination that has its origin in capitalism or patriarchy or racism and must be opposed with a single-minded democratic (or vanguardist) politics.[22] On the right, or some parts of the right, society is said to be one large exchange system, where autonomous individuals ought to be allowed to calculate their chances and maximize their values, without any sort of familial or communal, political or religious, interference.[23] Commodities, opportunities, capacities, places or positions of all sorts are, on this view, identical kinds of things, which individuals legitimately come to possess by paying the

---

[22] See the argument of Isaac D. Balbus, *Marxism and Domination* (Princeton, N.J.: Princeton University Press, 1982).

[23] A useful example of this sort of market imperialism is Gary Becker, *The Economic Approach to Human Behavior* (Chicago: University of Chicago Press, 1976).

market price—and in no other way. There are, no doubt, other doctrines that assert (or seek to recover) the unity of social life, but these are the two doctrines most familiar to us. Both their defenders and opponents are likely to believe that these two exhaust the range of contemporary possibility. One: if we don't organize a political challenge to, say, capitalist domination, the rulers of the market will rule everywhere. Two: if we don't uphold the free market in social goods, we will end up in servitude to the state or the party.

V

Behind these two totalizing views of society, we can glimpse something else: two visions of human wholeness. On the one hand, the ideal human being is the citizen, a radically political person, active and engaged, sovereign over all distributive decisions, even though this sovereignty must be shared with the body of citizens and exercised collectively. On the other hand, the ideal human being is the rational maximizer, a radically autonomous individual, calculating, risk-taking, who makes his or her distributive decisions alone, even though these are subject to the impersonal coordination of the market. What both these views share is the sense that the self is or ought to be one self, unified and single-minded in all its transactions. Insofar as this self acknowledges different sorts of goods, it always does so in the same way: making its choices under the aegis of a political ideology or an individualized hierarchy of value.

But these are, both of them, radically minimalist accounts of the human person. They derive their (real but limited) critical force from the experience of societies where democratic decision making has been repressed or devalued or confined to a privileged group or where market exchange has been coercively controlled by local authorities or planned and directed by the central state. In such cases, it is relatively easy to see the point of the demand for political or economic rights. But neither of these demands represents the be-all or end-all of human liberation. The rights in question are rights to act within a sphere (the sphere of politics has a specially extended form, but I will leave that aside for now) in ways appropriate to that sphere. The two modes of action—politics and exchange—draw on some of the interests and capacities of the self as we understand it, but they don't by any means exhaust those interests and capacities. In fact, the self is as differentiated as the society in which it participates. The production of difference in both self and society is the dominant feature of, though it is certainly not unique to, modern history. Contemporary theories of citizenship and rational choice that ignore the differences or deny their value ought, therefore, to be rejected.

Plato's observation that tyranny in society makes for, and is the work of, a tyrannical self has ramifications far beyond the political sphere.[24] Plutocrats and meritocrats, as I have already suggested, are tyrants as much as autocrats are, and their personalities are distorted in comparable ways. In all three cases the self is dominated by a single set of interests and qualities. It may be that this domination is functional to certain sorts of worldly success (though Plato didn't think so). Hence the stark alternative posed by the Irish poet, William Butler Yeats:

> The intellect of man is forced to choose
> Perfection of the life, or of the work.[25]

The second perfection requires, on this view, a terrible one-sidedness; the first allows for a many-sided development of the self—as in the aristocratic ideal of the Renaissance. If

---

[24] Plato, *The Republic* VIII: 566–569.
[25] Yeats, "The Choice."

this is right, then we would have to pay a price for complex equality: the refusal to assign the full range of social goods on the basis of a single talent or a single achievement, in the state or the market or the arts and sciences, would deprive us of some great and glorious achievements. But it would also free us from the domination of tyrannical selves.

I suppose that tyrannical selves have a relatively easy time planning their careers. Unjust societies make for simplified projects, since they hold forth the promise that success in winning one social good can be converted into general success—a triumphant parade through all the spheres. But this triumph can only be achieved at the expense of other people seeking other, valued but nondominant, goods. A just society, by contrast, makes for complicated life plans, in which the self distributes itself, as it were, among the spheres, figuring simultaneously as a loving parent, a qualified worker, a committed citizen, an apt student, a discerning critic, a faithful member of the church, a helpful neighbor. No doubt, it is easy to imagine people distributing themselves in this way and earning, as it were, less complementary adjectives. I mean only to argue that we are more likely to aim at these different qualities if we are sure that intrinsic or at least different rewards are available for each of them—and no single convertible reward available for any one of them.

VI

Is complex equality a descriptive or a prescriptive morality? Does it gain thickness only by surrendering critical force? I hope to answer these questions in my third chapter, but it will be useful to anticipate that answer here. Certainly, complexity is in one sense descriptive; it mirrors the conventional values of helpfulness, faithfulness, critical discernment, and so on. It represents theoretically the actual pluralism of social goods and distributive principles and processes. It defends difference in a differentiated society. But since these "conventional" values are commonly neglected and frequently disparaged, and since this "actual" pluralism is often overridden and difference often tyrannically repressed, complexity is also, simultaneously, a critical standard. And the theory is a mirror in this second sense, that we see in it the real failures of our society and ourselves.

Here is another way in which distributive justice, properly understood, is a maximalist morality. Every maximalism stands in an intimate descriptive/critical relation with its own society. For what it expresses in its idiomatic, particularist, and circumstantial style is the socially constructed idealism of *these* people. It describes the things they make and value and distribute among themselves and the personal qualities that they cultivate and mean to respect, even if they most often fail to respect them, in the course of the distributions. Minimalism, by contrast, is a simplified and singleminded morality. It works with an elementary and undifferentiated understanding of society and self, abstracted from all the actual and elaborated understandings. A minimalist view is a view from a distance or a view in a crisis, so that we can recognize injustice only in the large. We can see and condemn certain sorts of boundary crossings, gross invasions of the domestic sphere, for example, like the appearance of the secret police in the middle of the night. But we won't have much to say about the precise boundaries of the home and the family or the character of legitimate action within the kinship system (or anywhere else). Minimalism gives us no access to the range of social meanings or the specific forms of distributive complexity. We can deal justly, as agents of distribution and as critics-in-detail, only from the inside of a maximalist morality.

THREE: *Maximalism and The Social Critic*

I

I have written two books on social criticism, and I am not sure that I have much left to say.[26] But I will try here to describe, more explicitly than I have yet done, how criticism works from within a particularist and therefore maximalist theory of distributive justice. For it has been a common reproach to *Spheres of Justice*—to the argument that distributive standards are internal to a culture—that it precludes serious or radical social criticism. This is a worrisome matter: for my purpose in writing the book, to paraphrase Shakespeare's *Othello*, was nothing if not critical.[27]

The best way to begin is to suggest the natural or, at least, the most obvious form of internal or "immanent" criticism. I think that this is also the most common form of criticism generally, not only of institutions and practices but also of individual behavior. It's not my purpose here to address the question of individuals, but it is worth noting the extent to which social criticism works from what might be called the private or personal analogy. We often criticize friends and colleagues for not living up to a set of

---

[26] *Interpretation and Social Criticism; The Company of Critics: Social Criticism and Political Commitment in the Twentieth Century* (New York: Basic Books, 1988).

[27] "Do not put me to't/For I am nothing if not critical," *Othello* II.i.

41

standards that we and they profess to honor. We measure them against their own pretended ideals; we charge them with hypocrisy or bad faith. A critic who holds up a mirror to society as a whole is engaged in a similar enterprise. He means to show us *as we really are,* and what gives this demonstration its moral force, what makes the mirror a critical instrument inspiring dismay and guilt, is a pervasive and profound social idealism. Individuals need to maintain a high opinion of themselves, a sense of their probity and righteousness; and similarly the members of any society (especially the leading members) need to believe that their distributive arrangements and policies are just. Hence the lies they tell, not only to others but also to themselves, their everyday evasions, and the veil they draw over the more ugly features of the world they have made. The critic tears aside the veil.

The need for self-justification has, no doubt, a number of reasons; we can give both cynical and sympathetic accounts of it. Why did the pharaohs of ancient Egypt, for example, or the kings of Babylonia and Assyria, in the earliest inscriptions, proclaim their commitment to seeing justice done, the poor sustained, widows and orphans protected?[28] Was it because they thought that their power would be more secure if their subjects believed in the commitment? Or because their own self-esteem depended on thinking themselves committed? Or because the rituals of commitment (and then the inscriptions) were required by the gods? Or because this was what the rulers of states had always said about themselves? (But why had they said it?) It doesn't matter. If the pharaoh promises that he will see justice done, then the way is open for some Egyptian scribe to take his courage in his hands and

---

[28] H. W. F. Saggs, *Civilization Before Greece and Rome* (New Haven, Conn.: Yale University Press, 1989), chapter 8.

write out a catalogue of all the injustices the pharaoh in fact condones.

But this kind of criticism, though brave enough, is limited by the reigning or conventional ideals. What if the scribe wants to criticize the conventions? It's not likely that he means to deny that justice ought to be done. Perhaps he has some new vision of what justice entails. If the new vision is to be persuasive, however, it will have to be connected by argument to the old one. Sustaining the poor with royal charity, the scribe might say, brings no end to poverty; what is needed instead is an agrarian law, a division of the land. (It will matter, of course, how the land is understood. Is it a gift of the gods? To whom? For what purpose?) Or perhaps the scribe believes that this pharaoh, or pharaohs generally, will never live up to the conventional commitments: what is needed is priestly or, even better, scribal rule. I don't know of any Egyptian scribes who made arguments of this sort; I only want to insist that they are possible arguments. They start from the existing social idealism and claim that the ideals are hypocritically held, or ineffectively enforced by the powers that be, or inadequate in their own terms.

Consider a better known, more extensively documented, example: the critique of hierarchy in medieval and early modern Europe. Here there was (what probably also existed in the ancient world) a complex and internally divided ideological system. I will mark off, schematically, only two forms of justification: religious and secular, Christian and feudal. Hierarchy had, of course, its religious defense and its clerical defenders, but Christianity was also always at least potentially subversive, its biblical texts suggesting a kind of primitive or original egalitarianism:

> When Adam delved and Eve span,
> Who was then the gentleman?

But I want to focus here on feudal ideology, hierarchical from start to finish, though not without its own critical potential. For it was the claim of the gentlemen, lords, and barons who occupied each hierarchical rank, that they served the ranks below. Service was the social ideal of the feudal system; its founding myth was a tale of the strong defending the weak.[29] The usual crowd of scribes, lay or clerical, provided the usual mapping out of the ideal in terms of justice done and protection provided. And when justice was not done and protection not provided, an occasional critic appeared to castigate a dissolute and degenerate aristocracy.

But criticism of this sort, it might be said again, in fact upholds the system, for it is addressed only to deviant individuals or groups. The bad aristocrats are castigated, while aristocracy itself is celebrated and the ideal of service reaffirmed. So they are; but the celebration is subversive insofar as the aristocratic ideal is distinguished from every actual instance of aristocratic behavior. Soon some bolder critic will ask why it is that these lordly and privileged men so rarely perform the services that supposedly justify their position. The revolutionary critique of artistocrats as parasites has its origin here: they have work to do but don't do it![30]

Hierarchy is a distributive system in which place, standing, and role are thickly intertwined—in discourse, not necessarily in practice. Or, perhaps, necessarily not in practice, for pride of place undercuts the willingness to serve. Aristocrats find other roles—leisure, display, wit, intrigue—with far less cultural legitimacy. Thus the bold lines of Beaumarchais' Figaro: "Nobility, fortune, rank, position! How proud they make a man feel! What have

---

[29] Georges Duby, *The Three Orders: Feudal Society Imagined*, trans. Arthur Goldhammer (Chicago: University of Chicago Press, 1980), esp. chapters 5, 13, 22.

[30] The Abbé Sieyès, *What is the Third Estate?* trans. M. Blondel (London: Pall Mall Pres, 1963), chapter 1.

you done to deserve such advantages? Put yourself to the trouble of being born—nothing more!"[31] A helpful or protective lord or baron is now seen as a contradiction in terms (much like a benevolent despot—the adjective is readily deployed against the noun). And then there is no way to justify hierarchical standing. The whole structure collapses. I would suggest that the egalitarian doctrine of "the rights of man" was the product of, or was made possible by, this collapse. The feudal fortress was not stormed from without until it had been undermined from within. Or, to shift the metaphor, equality grows out of the critique of a failed hierarchy.[32]

Something similar could be said, I think, about the example with which I began my first chapter. How did the Czechs, and other East European dissidents, go about criticizing communism? Here too there existed a complex ideological culture, and it seems likely that a certain kind of criticism, and with it an elaborate pattern of evasion and resistance, was sustained from the beginning in religious and nationalist terms. This was mostly a submerged and clandestine critique, however, expressed only in private, to family and friends. It would be worth investigating in detail how criticism of this kind actually works under conditions of tyrannical repression; the crucial point, however, is that it does work. It even affects the distribution of such social goods as it can still (at least partially) control—recognition and honor, for example. But

---

[31] Beaumarchais, *The Barber of Seville and The Marriage of Figaro*, trans. John Wood (Harmondsworth: Penguin Books, 1964). *Marriage*, Act V, p. 199.

[32] Michel Foucault's argument for a radical and pretty much incomprehensible break between one *épistème* and its chronological successor (*The Order of Things*, trans. Alan Sheridan [New York: Pantheon, 1972]), whatever its value in intellectual history generally, doesn't seem to fit the history of political and social criticism.

the most dangerous criticism, which tyrants fear more than any other, is the criticism shaped not by old loyalties and ideologies but by their own putative idealism. The primary critics of communism, who opened the way for nationalists and Christians, were dissident communists, demanding that the tyrants actually deliver on the values to which they claimed to be committed (and to which their critics were really committed): freedom, equality, and democratic government.

The critique of communist tyranny no doubt also reflected a reiterated minimalism—hence our own instant solidarity with it. But this solidarity had its limits, for the full program of the earliest dissidents was a communist, even a Leninist, program that could not have been endorsed by many of their Western sympathizers.[33] Indeed, the full program lost much of its relevance, even for its Eastern sympathizers, as soon as the communist regimes collapsed, so much was it, if not a function of the regimes themselves, a product of the movements and ideology out of which the regimes had come. By that time, however, many of the dissidents had revised their critique, introducing new distinctions into the social idealism of the left. They came to believe that a state committed, even hypocritically, to simple equality and radical redistribution was necessarily too powerful, a threat to every other aspect of its own (putative) idealism, beyond reform. They became critics of Leninism as well as of Stalinism (and all the local imitations of Stalinism), and so drew closer to what we can think of as the standard maximalist morality of the West: liberalism, democracy, "bourgeois civil rights." But it was the experience of internal dissidence, and the recognition

---

[33] See the account of earlier Polish (and Czech) dissidents by Adam Michnik, *Letters from Prison and Other Essays*, trans. Maya Lotynski (Berkeley: University of California Press, 1985).

of the extreme unlikelihood of reform from within, that led the critics to adopt this external model. Though the time span is much shorter, as befits the rhythms of modernity, the case is the same in the contemporary East as in the late medieval and early modern West. Liberalism grew out of the critique of a failed communism.

I have used these examples to suggest the radical potential of an internal critique: the subversiveness of immanence. Social criticism in maximalist terms can call into question, can even overturn, the moral maximum itself, by exposing its internal tensions and contradictions. And this seems to me the normal course of criticism even when the critics don't mean to run the full length of the course, aiming at reform or reconstruction, say, rather than at subversion. Social critics commonly start from where they stand, win or lose on their own ground.

II

But how—so the critic of *Spheres of Justice* commonly continues—can this original, normal, internal criticism ever find persuasive expression?[34] I think that this question has a very particular point: what is being asked is how internal criticism can ever find a definitive philosophical expression. For the claims that the dissidents make about communist freedom and equality (or the claims they make about feudal service and protection) are always disputed. And there are alternative accounts of vanguard tyranny (and aristocratic privilege): more or less credible stories that can also be given a historical

---

[34] See Ronald Dworkin, "To Each His Own," *New York Review of Books*, April 14, 1983, pp. 4–6, and the subsequent exchange between Dworkin and myself, *NYRB* July 21, 1983, pp. 43–46.

dimension and rooted in old texts. So the internal criticism, as long as it is confined to the interpretation of communism (or feudalism) as a maximalist morality, always falls short—not only as a practical but even as a theoretical endeavor. People who live inside the moral/ cultural thickness of the old regime, who read these books, obey (or evade) these laws, celebrate this tradition, and so on, nonetheless disagree about what it all "means." The result is an intellectual as well as a political stalemate. And then the only thing to do, at the end, after all the possibilities of interpretive criticism have been exhausted—so say the critics of immanence—is to appeal to an external standard: the best abstract and general theory that deals with the matters in dispute.

Of course, if one really were in secure possession of the best abstract and general theory, one probably wouldn't bother with internal criticism at all. All the local critics could be replaced by a universal Office of Social Criticism, where an internationally recruited and specially trained civil service (of professional philosophers? political theorists? theologians?) applied the same moral principles to every country, culture, and religious community in the world. I would not be surprised if the medieval Church and the old Comintern had such offices, under different names. And there may well be organizations aspiring to this status today, attached to the United Nations or independently constituted. But if the aim here is maximalist in character—to render a detailed judgment of moral values and social practices everywhere—then theoretical possession is as likely as interpretive understanding to be disputed. The leap from inside to outside, from the particular to the general, from immanence to transcendence, changes the terrain of the argument, but I know of no evidence that the argument marches more readily toward closure on its new terrain. Even people who read the same books (of moral philosophy, say) are likely to disagree about which abstract and general theory is really the best.

It is still possible, as I argued in the first chapter, to move effectively from the particular to the general—as when a group of critics give up their own maximalism and embrace (or invent) for some specific purpose a moral minimum. This is, I think, the approach of groups like Amnesty International, which can certainly play a useful critical role—so long as they restrain whatever impulse their members have to impose a complete set of moral principles across the range of cultural difference. Success depends upon this self-restraint, for otherwise Amnesty International would represent one more missionizing maximalism, like the Church and the Comintern. Its members would make themselves into a kind of global vanguard, aspiring, perhaps, to rule outside their sphere, claiming political authority everywhere on the basis of ideological correctness. If, however, there is (as I believe) no single, correct, maximalist ideology, then most of the disputes, and certainly most of the distributive disputes, that arise within a particular society and culture have to be settled— there is no choice—from within. Not without suggestions from the outside, not without reference to other maximal moralities, but by and large through the kind of interpretive arguments that I described in my last chapter and through political processes adjusted to them. Social critics mostly work out of a Home Office.

All this is not to say that moral maximalism can't be "theorized"—first of all in a general way and then more particularly. We can explain its general value and the deference we owe to each of its particular versions (and the limits of that deference). And then we can try to specify its content in some particular case and for some particular purpose, giving a theoretical account of local justice, for example, displaying the interconnections of its various parts and defending a view of its priorities. To construct a theory out of an actual thick morality is mostly an interpretive (rather than a philosophically creative) task. If the purpose is critical, then what is required is a *pointed* interpretation, a localized theory that concludes with a moral maxim—the philosophical equivalent of an Aesopian fable. Indeed, it is a good thing if the interpreter is able to tell a story, making his critical argument from within a tradition, acknowledging the significance of historical events and proper names even as he reaches for the appropriate theoretical terms.

III

But doesn't this account (I am still following in the tracks of my critics) miss the excitement and heroism of the critical enterprise?[35] My imaginary Egyptian scribe takes his life in his hands; the early Czech dissidents put their careers and their own and their family's safety on the line. How could they do this unless they were sure that they had gotten things right—not only that their interpretation of the maximalist morality was the one true interpretation but also that this maximalist morality was the one true morality? I have been talking about a thin universalism and a thick particularism, but isn't criticism at its most powerful when it claims to be both thick and universal, rich in its detail, expansive in its scope—a full philosophical account of the right and the good? Think of Martin Luther as a critic of the Church: his critique was certainly based on an interpretation of Christian maximalism about which he had no doubts (it wasn't just one possible interpretation). And the argument had universal reach: everyone should be or become a Christian of the Lutheran sort. If Luther had not believed this, could he have been so strong, so confident of where he stood and what he could and could not do?

---

[35] George Steiner, "Putting critics in their places," *Sunday Times Books* (London), 12 March 1989.

I am sure that Luther was a strong man and a great critic, but he was also brutal and intolerant—in part, at least, because of his Christian universalism. Nor is he the only model of the critic as hero; it would not be difficult to describe alternative models, critical styles more skeptical or more modest (as I have done, in fact, in *The Company of Critics*). But I want to attempt a different argument here; I want to deny that the critical enterprise is best understood with reference to its heroic moments. A recent and very fine book by two French scholars, Luc Boltanski and Laurent Thévenot, provides the sociological grounding of my argument: they have shown, precisely and in great detail, how ordinary an activity criticism is and how it necessarily works from within the different spheres of everyday life.[36] It reflects the full range of social differentiation; its various vocabularies are widely known; it is an activity of the many, not the special task of the few, and so it is carried out sometimes with wit, sometimes with vulgarity, skillfully and clumsily, bravely and timidly. No doubt, critics, like lovers, friends, and political militants, must sometimes act boldly and take risks. But their everyday story is different, closer to what I have called "common complaint" than high philosophical or theological argument. What's at stake is not the universal good or the divine will, but justice or liberty more locally understood.

Philosophical and theological critics do indeed have more far-reaching ambitions; hence the readiness with which they adopt heroic postures. In a sense, each one hopes to be the last social critic. If he gets things right, all that will ever be necessary in the future is the reprinting and the endless study of his texts. After all, the objects of critical scrutiny don't change all that much: human greed, cruelty, and lust; the abuse of power; the oppression of the

---

[36] Luc Boltanski and Laurent Thévenot, *De la Justification: Les économies de la grandeur* (Paris: Gallimard, 1991).

weak. Shouldn't it be possible to find the right response to all this, "the correct ideological position," so that no one would ever have to look again?

Yes, it is possible, but only in a minimalist way, responding to the grossest and most offensive injustices. But critics also respond to ordinary injustice, and they respond in detail, thickly and idiomatically. When they do that, criticism is a different sort of activity than its philosophical and theological heroes suggest. Of course, the critics try to get things right, just as I am trying to do now, but we ought to understand this effort less by analogy with what philosophers do than by analogy with what poets, novelists, artists, and architects do. No architect, for example, aims to design the last building (not even the last church or school) and make architecture henceforth unnecessary—even though he aims to get his particular building right. Rightness is relative to the architectural occasion: the needs that the building is intended to serve, the materials at hand, the reigning aesthetic idealism (the architectural equivalent of a maximalist morality). Architecture is a reiterative activity, where many architects design many buildings, and it is in principle possible for all of them to get their designs right—though this doesn't mean that they all design the same perfect building. In practice, of course, they all produce imperfect buildings: more or less beautiful, habitable, useful. And each of these buildings immediately becomes an object of critical reflection and debate—models for the future that are imitated or revised or rejected. Indeed, they are imitated *and* revised *and* rejected, in endlessly reiterated architectural efforts with endlessly differentiated results. (Perhaps a minimalist universalism also develops, an international style—in hotel design, say—though this is unlikely to reflect the best architectural work.)

Criticism is also a reiterative activity, and the critics who aim to get things right aim at a rightness that is relative to their critical occasions. They want to produce a strong argument and a local political effect, but also, again, an object of reflection and debate—so that other critics are drawn into the argument (even though they know that these others won't piously repeat their own strictures). Let me try now to describe how they might go about doing this. What is the critical enterprise like, in its ordinary form, expressed in the idiom of a particular morality?

IV

Consider the political culture of the contemporary West, our own morally maximalist account of how power should be distributed. I will work out of the specifically American version of this account—more "federalist" than "republican," but, so far as my purposes go right now, not all that different from other Western versions. The basic principle that governs distributions in the sphere of politics is that power can legitimately be attained and held and used only with the consent of the governed. The principle is much older than modern democracy; it is a feature of medieval monarchy too, where the rulers themselves or their taxes or military mobilizations commonly required the consent of at least some of their subjects—for example, the barons, lords, and gentlemen. What the democratic revolutions accomplished, most importantly, was the replacement of "some" by "all." It is not surprising that the ideal citizen of early modern political theory is modeled on the renaissance and neo-classical ideal of the aristocrat. The citizen, né everyman, took over from the aristocrat the rights that made his and, later on, her consent meaningful—took over also the social space and the range of activities within which consent could be expressed. Hence the rights of petition and assembly, which the aristocracy had always held; the new right of a free press, made necessary by the creation of a mass public; and the rights of domestic and religious privacy, manifest in the aristocratic great houses and private chapels that kings invaded at their peril. The maxim that a man's home is his castle was originally defended by men whose castles were their homes. In the American colonies and then in the new republic, there was, of course, no native aristocracy, but the citizen was still conceived in this image of personal "liberty" and many-sided activism.

In an important sense, the principle of consent establishes a proceduralist ethic. It describes how one comes legitimately to exercise political power. Once the procedures are in place—periodic elections, freely organized parties, laws against the sale and purchase of votes, and so on—we commonly assume the legitimacy of the elected rulers. But this is much too narrow an understanding of democratic politics. In fact, what makes the proceduralism *proceed*, what gives it its legitimizing force, is a certain spirit, expressed in a set of practices.[37] The spirit is one of active engagement, and the practices include arguing, organizing, assembling, demonstrating, and petitioning as well as voting. Sometimes this sort of thing is simply assumed—as in the American Bill of Rights: when one asserts "the right of the people peacefully to assemble," one expects . . . assemblies. It would be a very bad sign were the "people" never to exercise their right. Precisely for this reason, democracy is characterized by a series of explicit efforts to create and sustain an active citizenry. (This is the central point of Rousseau's political theory, in which the neo-classical picture of the citizen is always explicit.) In the United States, public education is the most important of these efforts. The long debate about how to "Americanize" the immigrants was largely governed by the

---

[37] Cf. the argument of Robert Putnam, *Making Democracy Work: Civic Traditions in Modern Italy* (Princeton, N.J.: Princeton University Press, 1993).

same purpose—though the "Americanizers" were as often nativists as republicans.[38]

But this focus on citizenship is, in the American case, neither exclusive nor singular in character. It is a crucial feature of our political idealism that the commitment to democratic procedures, and then to the spirit and practices that they require, encompasses all levels of our federalist government and spills over into civil society. Much of the political education of American citizens takes place in the smallest political units that they inhabit—boroughs, townships, school districts—and then in churches, unions, philanthropic organizations, and so on. This process moves in two directions: if the citizens learn something about the uses and misuses of power, local governments and secondary associations are at the same time made more democratic. Or, at least, they are brought under democratic scrutiny. Though not often run in strict accordance with the principles of consent and participation, they are always subject to challenge in the name of those principles. Citizenship takes on a range of added and more particularized meanings: in the neighborhood, or in the community of the faithful, or in the labor movement, or among men and women committed to this philanthropy or that good cause.

Rousseau defines a virtuous citizen as one who "flies to the assemblies," meaning, to the assemblies of citizens.[39] Today we are more likely to give that definition a pluralist twist: many different assemblies, reflecting the material and ideal interests of different, though overlapping, groups of citizens. Virtue is still best displayed, I suppose, at

[38] For a discussion of American "republicanism," see Michael Walzer, *What It Means to be an American* (New York: Marsilio, 1993), pp. 23ff. and 81ff.

[39] Jean-Jacques Rousseau, *The Social Contract*, Bk. III, chapter XV.

meetings, but this is not necessarily the sort of virtue that produces a Rousseauian general will. What is virtuous is the activity (and the spirit that animates and infuses it), not the outcome of the activity—itself, often enough, decidedly unsatisfactory. We aim to give this activity maximum scope. Hence, the claim of the Italian political theorist Norberto Bobbio that the the critical question for democrats is not whether the citizens vote, or exactly how many of them vote, but *where* they vote—this claim applies with special force to the American experience.[40] Many issues, many settings, much consenting and refusing: this is our ideal picture of democratic politics.

But this picture must not be overdrawn; it cannot obscure all the other pictures of social activity in a differentiated society inhabited by "many-sided" men and women. Power is not always at issue; nor is consent the only distributive principle. So political virtue is tempered by what we can think of as apolitical virtue, itself of many different sorts: familial love, professional competence, even the "green thumb" that rules the market. There are indeed places where citizens need not vote, and social critics are obliged to fit their democratic arguments into a larger view of distributive complexity. They have nonetheless a powerful weapon in their hands: a thick, internalist account of how one crucially important social good ought to be distributed, an account that is culturally warranted and at odds with every actual distribution.

I want to stress that though this account starts with simple equality (one citizen/one vote), its aim is to justify inequality. The way one wins unequal power—to hold or control a state office or to carry out a policy, say—is to persuade one's fellow citizens to agree to the inequality: one

---

[40] Norberto Bobbio, *Democracy and Dictatorship*, trans. Peter Kennealy (Minneapolis: University of Minnesota Press, 1989), p. 157.

must first win an argument and then an election. But this short list of necessary victories is too short. Democratic politics, even in its ideal form, is only in part argumentative; it is also a matter of organization, bargaining, strategy, demonstrations of strength, and much else. In all this, power is exercised even as it is pursued, and it is always a difficult question how the exercise can be brought under the rule of consent.

Despite the difficulty, we can see readily enough how a critique of American politics could be developed from this thick account of democratic idealism. The critique would have a twofold focus. It would aim first at exposing the most important kind of distributive aggression in American society: the invasion of the political sphere by wealthy individuals or by the masters of corporate wealth. This is not always or everywhere the most important (or the most effective) kind of aggression: think of how long it took the West European bourgeoisie to displace the old aristocrats from the political sphere or how easily its Eastern counterparts were themselves displaced by party militants and state bureaucrats. But the power of wealth is certainly characteristic of contemporary America—and because it is characteristic, it has its own local ideological justifications. So the democratic idea must be articulated with these in mind, *against them*, showing in specific ways, with concrete examples, how state power is seized and used even though the consent of those subject to it is never asked. A book like Charles Lindblum's *Politics and Markets* provides a good academic model of this critical enterprise; it is a sad commentary on the quality of American political life today that there are no very good popular models.[41]

---

[41] Charles Lindblum, *Politics and Markets: The World's Political-Economic Systems* (New York: Basic Books, 1977); see also the earlier work of

Democratic criticism would aim, secondly, at revising the internal boundaries of American society—exposing the exercise of something very much like political power outside the recognized political sphere, beyond the reach of the principle of consent. Here there are a number of different targets, each with its own ideological defenses, which need to be addressed one by one: the despotism of factory managers and corporate executives, the autocracy of university presidents, the patriarchal absolutism of male "heads of households," and so on. The argument is similar in each case but by no means the same. The more like political power these are, the more they should be subjected to democratic rules. But these rules will have to be qualified or revised in accordance with our understanding of the relevant goods at stake in the different spheres—in markets, commodities; in schools, learning; in families, mutual affection and the socialization of children. With regard to the last of these, feminist literature provides both popular and academic examples of the form and style of democratic criticism; among American texts, I would recommend especially Susan Okin's *Justice, Gender, and the Family*.[42]

V

It should be clear that this kind of criticism, calling for the realization of democratic idealism here and now, is not a defense of democracy itself. This is not to say that democracy can't be defended; we have reasons for preferring it. But I take that question to be settled—for us at least—and begin instead with a series of interpretive claims about the meaning of the settlement. Yes, we are all democrats.

Grant McConnell, *Private Power and American Democracy* (New York: Knopf, 1966).
[42] Susan Moller Okin, *Justice, Gender, and the Family* (New York: Basic Books, 1989).

What follows from that commitment? What sort of life do democrats live when they are living in an authentically democratic way? Posing these questions does not preclude compromises of various sorts with other values, but it does suggest (what would have to be defended empirically and theoretically) that democracy has priority or at least special standing among contemporary American ideals. The adjectives are important—"contemporary," "American"—for it is clear, again, that this critique does not involve or require a defense of democracy in every time and place. It doesn't pretend to be an answer to the old Greek question about the best regime. That question has no singular and universal answer. What does the critic do, then, when he looks around and sees tyrannical governments in other countries, in distant places, and people marching in the street in opposition to their rulers—demanding not only "truth" and "justice" but also "democracy"?

I was ready, of course, to express my solidarity with the Chinese students in Tienanmen Square in 1989. But this readiness reflected a morally (and politically) minimalist position: solidarity with all the students, despite the disagreements among them, against the tyrants. I certainly did not believe then that American political idealism was about to be realized in China, or that it should be realized. Nor did I have an abstract and universal theory of "true democracy" to urge upon the Chinese. And I recognized in the arguments of the students—one had only to pay attention to what they were saying to Western journalists—a sense of their mission or their special political role that was clearly incompatible with the American ideal (in which a certain hostility to the claims of the educated classes has always been present) and probably incompatible too with the prevailing abstract and universal theories.[43] Student

---

[43] For the Americans, see Richard Hofstadter, *Anti-Intellectualism in American Life* (New York: Knopf, 1963).

elitism was rooted, perhaps, in Leninist vanguard politics or, more likely, in pre-communist cultural traditions (Confucian, mandarin) specific to China and certain to show up in any version of Chinese democracy. My solidarity with the students did not commit me to support their understanding of democratic government. My own (American) idealism did not commit me to oppose that understanding.

Watching from abroad, I could afford this benign disengagement, not from the political struggle as a whole but from its details. Were I to be invited to visit China and give a seminar on democratic theory, I would explain, as best I could, my own views about the meaning of democracy. But I would try to avoid the missionizing tone, for my views include the idea that democracy in China will have to be *Chinese*—and my explanatory powers do not reach to what that means. Indeed, it seems to me that this idea of local prerogative follows from what we might think of as moral minimalism in the international arena (the subject of my fourth chapter). The principle of consent requires this much at least: that Chinese democracy be defined by the Chinese themselves in terms of their own history and culture.

Against this argument, it might be said that I am allowing the (foreign) social critic to speak for some (perhaps mythical) version of collective China, the cultural tradition standardly understood, maybe even the old elites, but not for the individual and his or her rights. In one sense, this is clearly wrong, for I do defend the minimal rights of Chinese, as of Czech, demonstrators. But these are unknown and therefore abstract individuals: minimal rights are all they have. Rights-in-detail, rights thickly conceived, belong only to concrete men and women, who are, as Marx and Engels argued in their *German Ideology*, individuated in society.[44] Since I know very little about their society, I

---

[44] Karl Marx and Friedrich Engels, *The German Ideology*, Parts I and II, ed. R. Pascal (New York: International Publishers, 1947), "Feuerbach."

cannot foist upon the Chinese this or that set of rights—certainly not my own preferred set. So I defer to them as empirical and social individuals. They must make their own claims, their own codifications (a Chinese bill of rights?), and their own interpretative arguments.

Someday, no doubt, they will produce their own version of democratic politics, and then a controversy will develop over whether it should be more, or less, "participatory"—and perhaps I will join the controversy, not as a social critic, but simply as an interested student and sometime political theorist. But I have no reason to anticipate that argument now. All that my democratic idealism requires *now* is that I support the dissident students, encouraging them to make their own way, without worrying about whether their way will also be mine. There isn't much room for moral maximalism here. The work of the critic, when it is maximalist work, is also local and particularist in character.

It doesn't follow, however, that the character of these individuals is "entirely determined by the division of labor" (p. 65).

FOUR: *Justice and Tribalism:
Minimal Morality In
International Politics*

I

All over the world today, but most interestingly and
frighteningly in Eastern Europe and the former Soviet
Union, men and women are reasserting their local and
particularist, their ethnic, religious, and national identities. The tribes have returned, and the drama of their
return is greatest where their repression was most severe.
It is now apparent that the popular energies mobilized
against totalitarian rule, and also the more passive stub-
bornness and evasiveness that eroded the Stalinist regimes
from within, were fueled in good part by "tribal" loyalties
and passions. How these were sustained and reproduced
over time is a tale that waits to be told. The tribes—most
of them, at least, and all the minorities and the subject
nations—were for several generations denied access to the
official organs of social reproduction: the public schools
and the mass media. I imagine tens of thousands of old men
and women whispering to their grandchildren, singing folk
songs and lullabies, repeating ancient stories. This is in
many ways a heartening picture, for it suggests the in-
evitability of totalitarian failure. But what are we to make
of the songs and stories, often as full of hatred for neigh-
boring nations as of hope for national liberation? How
should we stand vis-à-vis the tribes?

Songs and stories are the expression of a thick moral
and political culture, to whose protagonists we are likely

63

to be sympathetic (as in the Czech example that shaped my first chapter) for thin or minimalist reasons: because we oppose the oppression, deceit, and torture that accompanied totalitarian rule. These reasons, however, can't be made to generate an alternative totality—the empire of reason, say. Ever since the Enlightenment, there has been a tendency, especially on the political left, to think that some rational and universal alternative must exist to both the tribes and their oppressors. But moral minimalism, while reasonable enough and universal enough, has no imperial tendencies; it doesn't aspire to global rule. It *leaves room* for all the tribes—and so for the particularist versions of justice and criticism that I have described. I want now to examine the character and the limits of this moral room. Sympathetic we may be, but we need not accept everything that we hear in the songs and stories of the old men and women.

The left has never understood the tribes.[45] Faced with their contemporary resurgence, its first response is to argue for their containment within established multi-national states—democratically transformed, of course, but not divided. This looks very much like a systematic repetition of the response of early twentieth-century social democrats to the nationalist movements that challenged the old empires. The "internationalism" of the left owes a great deal to Hapsburg and Romanov imperialism, even if leftists always intended to dispense with the dynasties. They were convinced that larger and more inclusive political units were always better. So many nations had lived together in

[45] For a standard Marxist account, see Eric Hobsbawm, "Some Reflections on 'The Break-up of Britain'" in *New Left Review* 105 (1977), pp. 3–23. The most interesting leftist discussions of nationalism are those of the Austrian Marxists Otto Bauer and Karl Renner: see *Austro-Marxism*, ed. and trans. Tom Bottomore and Patrick Goode (Oxford: Clarendon Press, 1978), Pt. III.

peace under imperial rule: why couldn't they continue to live together under the aegis of social democracy? So many nations lived together in peace under communist rule: why . . . ? When Western Europe is forging a new unity, how can anyone defend separation in the East?

But unity in the West is itself the product of or, at least, the historical successor to separation. The independence of Sweden from Denmark and, less than a century later, of Norway from Sweden (and of Finland from Sweden and Russia) opened the way for Scandinavian cooperation. The division of Belgium and Holland, and the failures of French imperialism, made possible the Benelux experiment. Centuries of sovereignty for the great states of Western Europe preceded the achievement of European community. It is important to note that what was achieved first, before community, was not only sovereign statehood but also democratic government. The Swedes could have held Norway indefinitely under one or another form of authoritarian rule. But mass mobilization and the practice of democracy, even in their earliest stages, made it clear that there was more than one *demos*, and then separation became necessary if democracy was to be sustained. The case is the same in the East. Multi-nationalism as it has existed there is a function of pre-democratic or anti-democratic politics. But bring the "people" into political life and they will arrive, marching in tribal ranks and orders, carrying with them their own languages, historical memories, customs, beliefs, and commitments—their own moral maximalism.[46] And once they have been summoned, once they have arrived, it isn't possible to do them justice within the old political order.

---

[46] See the argument about the effects of mass mobilization in Karl Deutsch, *Nationalism and Social Communication: An Inquiry into the Foundations of Nationality* (Cambridge, Mass.: M.I.T. Press, 1953).

Maybe it's not possible to do them justice at all. In Eastern Europe today, and in Caucasia, and in much of the Middle East, the prospects don't seem bright, given the sheer number of suddenly raucous tribes and the radical entanglement of their members on the same bits and pieces of land. Good fences make good neighbors only when there is some general agreement on where the fences should go. In the West, powerful states were created before the appearance of nationalist ideology and managed to repress and incorporate many of the smaller nations (Welsh, Scots, Normans, Bretons, and so on). The separations I have already noted took place alongside constructive processes that created large nation-states with more or less identifiable boundaries and more or less committed members. Similar efforts in Eastern Europe seem to have failed: there aren't many committed Yugoslav or Soviet citizens. The abandonment of these identities is startling in its scope and speed, and it leaves many people who had traveled under their protection suddenly vulnerable: Serbs in Croatia, Albanians in Serbia, Armenians in Azerbaijan, Russians in the Baltic states, Jews in Russia, and so on, endlessly.

There doesn't seem to be any humane or decent way to disentangle the tribes, and at the same time the entanglements are felt to be dangerous—not only to individual life, which is reasonable enough, but also to communal well-being. Demagogues exploit the hopes for national revival, linguistic autonomy, the free development of schools and media—all supposedly threatened by cosmopolitan or antinational minorities. And other demagogues exploit the fears of the minorities, defending ancient irredentisms and looking (like the Serbs in Croatia) for outside help. In such circumstances, it is hard to say what justice means, even in its most minimalist forms, let alone what policies it might require. Hence the impulse of the left, uncomfortable in any case with particularist passions, to cling to whatever unities exist and make them work. The argument is very much like that of a Puritan minister in the 1640s, defending the union of husband and wife against the new doctrine of divorce:

> If they might be separated for discord, some would make a commodity of strife; but now they are not best to be contentious, for the law will hold their noses together 'til weariness make them leave off struggling. . . .[47]

The problem, then as now, is that justice, whatever it requires, doesn't seem to permit the kinds of coercion that would be necessary to "hold their noses together." So we have to think about divorce, despite its difficulties. It is some help that divorce among nations needn't have the singular legal form of divorce in families. Self-determination for husbands and wives is relatively simple, even when important constraints are imposed upon the separated individuals. Self-determination for the many different kinds of tribes (nations, ethnic groups, religious communities) is bound to be more complicated, and the constraints that follow upon separation more various. There is room for maneuver.

II

I doubt that we can find a single rule or set of rules that will determine the form of the separation and the necessary constraints. But there is a general principle, which we can think of as the expression of moral minimalism in international politics. The principle is "self-determination." We will most readily understand it as a claim for democratic rights, and so it is in our time and place. But the principle has been reiterated in many different times and places,

---

[47] Henry Smith, quoted in C. L. Powell, *English Domestic Relations, 1487–1653* (New York: Columbia University Press, 1917), p. 75.

always in some local idiom and with a set of maximalist accompaniments. "Self-determination" is abstracted from all of its reiterations, including our own. When ancient Jews and Gauls defended their freedom against the Romans, the arguments they made were hardly democratic; nor were they cast in the language of rights.[48] But we have little difficulty recognizing the principle even in alien idioms. What was at stake for Jews and Gauls, what is at stake for us today, is the value of a historical or cultural or religious community and the political liberty of its members.

This value is not compromised, it seems to me, by the post-modern discovery that communities are social constructions: imagined, invented, put together out of a great variety of cultural and political materials. Constructed communities are the only communities there are, and so they can't be less real or less authentic than some other kind.[49] Their members, then, have the basic right that goes with membership. *They ought to be allowed to govern themselves* (in accordance with their own political ideas)— insofar as they can decently do that, given their local entanglements. Moral minimalism does not suggest a single best political unit. There is no ideal tribe; self-

---

[48] See the speeches of these ancient "nationalists" as reported by Julius Caesar in *War Commentaries*, trans. Rex Warner (New York: New American Library, 1960), pp. 29–30, 74, and by Josephus, *The Jewish War* VIII: 329–380.

[49] Hence Hobsbawm is surely wrong to argue that nations, because they are "imagined communities," serve ineffectively and inauthentically "to fill the emotional void left by the retreat or disintegration . . . of *real* human communities" (*Nations and Nationalism since 1780: Programme, Myth, Reality* [Cambridge: Cambridge University Press, 1990], p. 46, italics in original). Even small face-to-face communities, as anthropologists have taught us, are "imagined" in complex and elaborate ways.

determination has no absolute subject. Cities, nations, federations, immigrant societies—all these can be and have been governed by their own members. The contemporary tribes most certain of their unity, the obvious singularity of their identity and culture (the Poles or Armenians, say), are in fact historical composites. If we go back far enough in their history, we will find people's noses being held together (that's one of the methods of social construction). But if the descendants of these people, forgetting ancient indignities, regard themselves now as *fellow* members of a "community of character," within which they find identity, self-respect, and sentimental connections, why should we deny them the right of self-government?[50]

Except . . . unless . . . were it not for the fact that the self-government of tribe A, happily divorced, makes tribe B a vulnerable and unhappy minority in its own homeland. Locked into an independent Croatia, Serbs believe (not implausibly) that they will live in insecurity. And then, surely, the political unit has to be large, inclusive, undivided: all the tribes and fragments of tribes that live *here*—noses held together 'til they leave off struggling— must come under the authority of a neutral or thinly constituted state and share a citizenship that has no particular cultural character. But these can't be our only options: the dominance of one tribe or a common detribalization. For the second of the two, if it isn't a mere cover for the first, would require coercion of a sort that, as I have already suggested, is neither morally permissible nor politically effective. We would not be worrying about Croatia and its Serbs (or Bosnia and its Muslims or Serbia and its Albanians), if Yugoslavia had succeeded in imposing itself

---

[50] "Community of character" is Otto Bauer's phrase; see *Austro-Marxism*, p. 107.

upon its constituent nations; it was, in theory at least, the very model of a neutral state.

Neutrality is likely to work well only in immigrant societies where everyone has been similarly and in most cases voluntarily transplanted, cut off from homeland and history. In such cases—America is the prime example—tribal feelings are relatively weak. But how can one create a neutral state in France, say, where the anciently established French rule over the new immigrants from North Africa, exactly as they would have ruled over a French Union incorporating Algeria? What imperial, bureaucratic, or international authority could detribalize the French? Or the Poles in Poland? Or the Georgians in an independent Georgia? Or the Croats in Croatia? And then the only way to avoid domination is to multiply political units and jurisdictions, permitting a series of separations. But the series will be endless—so we are told—each divorce justifying the next one, smaller and smaller groups claiming the right of self-determination; and the politics that results will be noisy, incoherent, unstable, and deadly.

I want to argue that this is a slippery slope down which we need not slide (*need not:* I can't say will not). In fact, there are many conceivable arrangements between dominance and detribalization and between dominance and separation—and there are moral and political reasons for choosing different arrangements in different circumstances (for Algeria, say, and then for Algerians in France). The principle of self-determination is subject to interpretation and amendment. What has been called "the national question" doesn't have a single correct answer, as if there were only one way of "being" a nation, one version of national history, one model of relationships among nations. History reveals many ways, versions, and models, and so it suggests the existence of many more or less secure stopping points along the slippery slope. Consider now some of the more likely possibilities.

III

The easiest case is that of the "captive," that is, recently and coercively incorporated, nation—the Baltic states are nice examples, since these were sovereign nation-states, the nationality ancient even if statehood was only recently achieved and briefly held. The captivity was wrong for the same reasons that the capture was wrong. The principle involved is minimalist and familiar, declaring aggression anywhere in the world to be a criminal act. What it requires now is the restoration of independence and sovereignty—which is to say: what principle requires is what practice in this case has achieved. And by a kind of imaginative extension, we can grant the same rights to nations that *ought to have been* independent, where the solidarity of the group is plain to see and the crime of the ruling power is oppression rather than conquest. I see no reason to deny the justice of separation in all such cases.

Except . . . unless . . . Conquest and oppression are not merely abstract crimes; they have consequences in the real world: the mixing up of peoples, the creation of new and heterogeneous populations. Suppose that Russian immigrants now made up a majority of the people living in Latvia: would any right remain of Latvian self-determination? Suppose that French colonists had come (by 1950, say) to outnumber the Arabs and Berbers of Algeria: would the right of "Algerian" self-determination reside with the French majority? These are doubly hard questions; they are painful and they are difficult. The world changes, not necessarily in morally justifiable ways; and rights can be lost or, at least, diminished through no fault of the losers. We might want to argue for partition in cases like the ones I've just described, leaving the "natives" with less than they originally claimed; or we might want to design a regime of cultural autonomy instead of the political sovereignty that once seemed morally necessary. We look for the nearest possible arrangement to whatever was *ex ante* just, taking into account now what justice requires for the immigrants and colonists, or their children, who are not themselves the authors of the conquest or the oppression.

The case is the same with anciently incorporated nations—aboriginal peoples like the Native Americans or the Maori in New Zealand. Their rights too are eroded with time, not because the wrong done to them is wiped out (it may well grow greater, with ramifying and increasingly deleterious effects on their communal life), but because the possibility no longer exists for the restoration of anything remotely resembling their former independence. They stand somewhere between a captive nation and a national, ethnic, or religious minority. Something more than equal citizenship is due them, some degree of collective self-rule, but exactly what this might mean in practice will depend on the residual strength of their own institutions and on the character of their engagement in the common life of the larger society. They cannot claim any absolute protection against the pressures and attractions of the common life—as if they were an endangered species.[51] Confronted with modernity, all the human tribes are endangered species; their thick cultures are subject to erosion. All of them, whether or not they possess sovereign power, have been significantly affected. We can recognize what might be called a right to resist these effects, to build walls against contemporary culture, and we can give this right more or less scope depending on constitutional structures and local circumstances; we cannot guarantee the success of the resistance.

---

[51] Cf. Will Kymlicka's argument for the protection of minority cultures in *Liberalism, Community and Culture* (Oxford: Clarendon Press, 1991), esp. chap. 9.

IV

The just treatment of national minorities depends on two sets of distinctions: first, between territorially concentrated and dispersed minorities; and, second, between minorities radically different from and those that are only marginally different from the majority population. In practice, of course, both distinctions are really unmarked continuums, but it is best to begin with the clear cases. Consider, for example, a minority community with a highly distinctive history and culture and a strong territorial base—like the Albanians in Kosovo, for example. Their fellow nationals hold the adjoining state; they are trapped on the wrong side of the border as a result of some dynastic marriage or military victory long ago. The humane solution to their difficulty is to move the border; the brutal solution is to "transfer" the people; and the best practical possibility is some strong version of local autonomy, focused on cultural and educational institutions and the revenues that support them.

The opposite case is that of a marginally differentiated and territorially dispersed community, something like the ethnic and religious groups of North America (though there are exceptions in both categories: the ethnic French in Quebec, say, and the religious Amish in Pennsylvania). By and large, the experience of marginal difference and territorial dispersion gives rise to very limited claims on the state—a good reason for doubting the dangers of the slippery slope. A genuinely equal citizenship and the freedom to express their differences in the voluntary associations of civil society: this is what the members of such minorities commonly, and rightly, ask for. They may also seek some kind of subsidy from state funds for their schools, day care centers, old age homes, and so on. But that is a request that hangs more on political judgments than on moral principles. We will have to form an opinion about the inner strengths and weaknesses of the existing civil society. (A group that has been severely discriminated against, however, and whose access to resources is limited, does have a moral claim on the state.)

Once again, majorities have no obligation to guarantee the survival of minority cultures. They may well be struggling to survive themselves, caught up in a common competition against commercialism and international fashion. Borders provide only minimal protection in the modern world, and minorities within borders, driven by their situation to a preternatural closeness, may do better in sustaining a way of life than the more relaxed majority population. And if they do worse, that is no reason to come to their rescue; they have a claim, indeed, to physical but not to cultural security.

The adjustment of claims to circumstances is often a long and brutal business, but it does happen. We see it today, for example, in the geographically concentrated but only marginally different nations of Western Europe— Welsh, Scots, Normans, Bretons, and so on—whose members have consistently declined to support radical nationalist parties demanding independence and sovereign power. In cases like these, some sort of regional autonomy seems both to suit the people involved (small numbers of them—political, not ethnic or religious, minorities—always excepted) and to be politically and morally suitable. The case is the same with small or dispersed but significantly different populations, like the Amish or like orthodox Jews in the United States, who commonly aim at a highly localized and apolitical separatism: voluntarily segregated neighborhoods and parochial schools. This too seems to suit the people involved, and it is politically and morally suitable. But no minimalist account of justice can specify the precise form of these arrangements. In fact, the forms are historically negotiated, and they depend upon shared understandings of what such negotiations mean and how they work. The Welsh and Scots have had a hand in the development of British political culture, even if this is not quite the hand they think they ought to have had. Hence their ready adjustment to parliamentary politics. Both the Amish and the Jews have learned, and added to, the repertoire of American pluralism.

Arrangements of these sorts should always be allowed, but they can't be imposed. What has made *Great* Britain possible is probably the common Protestantism of its component nations. The effort to include the Irish failed miserably. More recently, the inclusion of the Slovenes in greater Yugoslavia seems to have failed for similar reasons. The case is the same for the failure of communist inter-nationalism in Poland and pan-Arabism in Lebanon. But I don't mean to argue that the religious differences crucial in all these cases necessarily make for separation. Some-times they do and sometimes they don't. The differences are different in each case. They have more to do with memory and feeling than with any objective measure of dissimilarity. That's why models like my own, based on such factors as territorial concentration and cultural differ-ence, can never be anything more than rough guides. We have to work slowly and experimentally toward arrange-ments that satisfy the members (not the militants) of this or that minority. There is no single correct outcome.

V

This experimental work is certain to be complicated by the unequal economic resources of the different tribes. It is obviously an incentive to divorce if one of the partners—a nation, say, industrially advanced or in control of mineral resources—can improve its position by walking away from the existing union. The other partners are left worse off, though some of them, at least, were never involved in any sort of national oppression. They will contest the divorce, but what they are probably entitled to, it seems to me, is the international equivalent of alimony and child support. Long established patterns of cooperation cannot be abruptly terminated to the advantage of the most advantaged partners. On the other hand, the partners are not bound to stay together forever—not if they are in fact different tribes, with different political and moral cultures, who meet the minimal standards for autonomy or independence.

Often enough, separatist movements in the economically advantaged provinces or regions of some established union do not meet those standards. The best example is the Katangan secession of 1961, inspired, it appears, by Belgian entrepreneurs and corporate interests, without locally rooted support or, at least, without any visible signs of national mobilization.[52] In such cases, it is entirely justifiable for unionist forces to resist the secession and to seek (and receive) international support. Obviously, there is such a thing as inauthentic tribalism: here, the manipulation of potential but not yet politically realized differences for economic gain. It doesn't follow, however, that every wealthy or resourceful tribe is inauthentic. And so there are also cases in which resistance to secession is not justified and should not be internationally supported— so long as some agreement can be negotiated that meets the interests of the people left behind. Their fear of impoverishment must be weighed against the fear of oppression or exploitation on the part of the seceding group or against its desire for cultural expression and political freedom.

---

[52] Conor Cruise O'Brien, *To Katanga and Back: A UN Case Study* (New York: Simon & Schuster, 1962).

VI

The dominant feeling that makes for national antago-
nism, the most important cause (not the only cause) of all
the tribal wars, is fear. Here I mean to follow an old argument first made in Thomas Hobbes's *Leviathan*, where it
forms part of the explanation for the "war of all against
all." Hobbes was thinking of the internal wars of late medieval "bastard feudalism" but also—more pertinently for our
purposes—of the religious wars of his own time. There are
always a few people, he writes, who "take pleasure in con-
templating their own power in acts of conquest." But the
greater number by far are differently motivated: they
"would be glad to be at ease within modest bounds."[53]
These ordinary men and women are driven to fight not by
their lust for power or enrichment, not by their bigotry or
fanaticism, but by their fear of conquest and oppression.
Hobbes argues that only an absolute sovereign can free
them from this fearfulness and break the cycle of threats
and "anticipations" (that is, pre-emptive violence). In fact,
however, what broke the cycle, in the case of the religious
wars, was not so much political absolutism as religious
toleration.

The two crucial seventeenth-century arguments against
toleration sound very familiar today, for they closely par-
allel the arguments against national separation and autonomy. The first of the two is the claim of the dominant
religious establishments to represent some high value—
universal truth or the divine will—that is certain to be
overwhelmed in the cacophony of religious dissidence.
And the second is the slippery slope argument: that the
dissidence will prove endless and the new sectarianism
endlessly divisive, split following split until the social order

---

[53] Thomas Hobbes, *Leviathan*, Pt. I, chapter xiii.

crumbles into incoherence and chaos. Certainly, toleration opened the way for a large number of new sects, though these have mostly flourished on the margins of more or less stable religious communities. But it also, and far more importantly, lowered the stakes of religious conflict: toleration made divisiveness more tolerable.[54] It solved the problem of fear by creating protected spaces for a great diversity of religious practices.

It seems to me that we should aim at something very much like this today: protected spaces of many different sorts matched to the needs of the different tribes. Rather than supporting the old unions, I would be inclined to support separation whenever separation is demanded by a political movement that, so far as we can tell, represents the popular will. Let the people go who want to go. Many of them won't go all that far. And if there turn out to be political or economic disadvantages in their departure, they will find a way to re-establish connections. Indeed, if some new union—federation or confederation—is our goal, the best way to reach it is to abandon coercion and allow the tribes first to separate and then to negotiate their own voluntary and gradual, even if only partial, incorporation in a community of interest. Today's European Community is a powerful example, which other nations will approach at their own pace.

But, again, one nation's independence may be the beginning of another nation's oppression. Reading the newspaper these days, it often seems that the chief motive for national liberation is not to free oneself from minority status in someone else's country but to acquire (and then mistreat) minorities of one's own—as if the standard rule

---

[54] See John Locke's anticipation of this result in *A Letter Concerning Toleration* (1689), ed. Patrick Romanell (Indianapolis: Bobbs-Merrill, 1950), pp. 52–53.

of inter-tribal relations is the very opposite of golden: do unto others what has been done unto you. Arguing for liberation, I have largely ignored the persistent failure of new nation-states to meet the minimal moral test: to recognize in the nation-that-comes-next the rights vindicated by their own independence.[55] I don't mean to underestimate the nastiness of tribal zealots. But weren't the zealots of the religious wars equally nasty? And their latter day descendants seem harmless enough—not particularly attractive, many of them, but also not very dangerous. Why shouldn't the same sequence, harmlessness following upon nastiness, hold for contemporary nationalists? Put them in a world where they are not threatened, and for how long will they think it in their interests to threaten others?

That at least is the Hobbesian argument. No doubt there are men and women in every tribe—Serbs and Croats; Latvians, Georgians, and Russians; Greeks and Turks; Israeli Jews and Palestinian Arabs—who take pleasure in acts of conquest, who aim above all to triumph over their neighbors and enemies. But these people will not rule in their own tribes if we can make it possible for their fellow-tribesmen to live "at ease within modest bounds." Every tribe within its own modest bounds: this is the political equivalent of toleration for every church and sect. What makes it possible—though still politically difficult and uncertain—is that the bounds need not enclose, in every case, the same sort of space.

Religious toleration, however, was enforced by the state, and the godly zealots were disarmed and disempowered by the political authorities. Tribal zealots, by contrast, aim precisely at empowerment; they hope to become political

---

[55] I elaborate on this "test" in "Nation and Universe," *The Tanner Lectures on Human Values* XI (Salt Lake City: Utah University Press, 1990), pp. 549–552.

authorities themselves, replacing the imperial bureaucrats who once forced them to live peacefully with their internal minorities. Who will restrain them after independence? Who will protect the Serbs in an independent Croatia or the Albanians in an independent Serbia? I have no easy answer to these questions. In a liberal democracy, national minorities can seek constitutional protection. But not many of the new nations are likely to be liberal, even if they achieve some version of democracy. The best hope for restraint lies, I think, in federal or confederal checks and balances and in international pressure—and, when absolutely necessary, forceful intervention—on behalf of the moral minimum. The nationality treaties of the interwar period were notable failures, but some measure of success in protecting minorities ought to be possible now that nation-states are more entangled with and dependent on one another. Suppose that the leaders of the European Community or the World Bank or even the United Nations were to say to every nation seeking statehood: we will recognize your independence, trade with you or provide economic assistance—but only if you find some way to accommodate the national minorities that fear your sovereign power. The price of recognition and aid is accommodation.

What form this accommodation might take is not a matter to be determined in any *a priori* way (I have to keep saying this because so many people are looking for a quick theoretical fix). It will depend on the political and moral culture of the new states and on a process of negotiation. Here the different maximal moralities must be allowed their appropriate room. Secession, border revision, federation, regional or functional autonomy, cultural pluralism: there are many designs for "a room of one's own," many political possibilities, and no reason to think that the choice of one of these in this or that case makes a similar choice necessary in all the other cases. As the examples I have cited from Western Europe suggest, choices are more likely to be determined by concrete circumstances than by abstract principles. What is required is an international consensus that validates a variety of choices, supporting any political arrangement that satisfies the tribes at risk.

VII

But there is no guarantee of satisfaction and, sometimes, watching the tribal wars, some of us may yearn for the uniform repressiveness of imperial or even totalitarian rule. For wasn't this repression undertaken in the name, at least, of universalism—and, in the case of the communists, of a thick morality ambitiously intended to replace every sort of moral particularism? And mightn't it have done that? Mightn't it have produced, had it only been sustained long enough, a genuine detribalization? And then we would look back and say that just as the absolutism of early modern monarchs was necessary to defeat the aristocracy and eliminate feudalism, so the absolutism of imperial and communist bureaucrats was necessary to overcome tribalism. Perhaps the bureaucracies collapsed too soon, before they could complete their "historical task."

But this line of argument repeats again the old left misunderstanding of the tribes. It is no doubt true that particular tribes can be destroyed by repression, if it is cruel enough and if it lasts long enough. The destruction of tribalism itself, however, lies beyond the reach of any repressive power. It is no one's "historical task." Feudalism is the name of a regime, and regimes can be replaced. Tribalism names the commitment of individuals and groups to their own history, culture, and identity, and this commitment (though not any particular version of it) is a permanent feature of human social life. The parochialism, the moral thickness, that it breeds is similarly permanent. It can't be overcome; it has to be accommodated, and therefore the crucial minimalist principle is that it must always be accommodated: not only my parochialism but yours as well, and his and hers in their turn.

When my parochialism is threatened, then I am wholly, radically parochial: a Serb, a Pole, a Jew (a black, a woman, a homosexual), and nothing else. But this is an artificial situation in the modern world (and perhaps in the past too). The self is more naturally divided; at least, it is capable of division and even thrives on it. In domestic society, this inner division is produced by social differentiation. In international society and in multi-national states, it is produced by cultural difference. Neither of these is in any way simple (the divisions of the self are the subject of my last chapter). One line on the social or political map doesn't make for singular selves on either side; there are always cross-cutting lines. Under conditions of security, I will acquire a more complex identity than the idea of tribalism suggests. I will identify myself with more than one tribe, adding to the social construction of identity my own personal construction. Indeed, the experience of difference, when it is peaceful, increases the power of the individual subject, who maneuvers among a range of alternatives without ever being locked into a single one. So I can choose to be an American, a Jew, an Easterner, an intellectual, a professor. Imagine a similar multiplication of identities around the world, and the world begins to look like a less dangerous place. When identities are multiplied, passions are divided.

We need to think about the political structures best suited to this multiplication and division. These won't be unitary structures; nor will they be identical. Some states will be rigorously neutral, with a plurality of cultures and a common citizenship; some will be federations; some will be nation-states, with minority autonomy. Sometimes cultural pluralism will be expressed only in private life; sometimes it will be expressed publicly. Sometimes different tribes will be mixed on the ground; sometimes they will be territorially grouped. Since the nature and number of our identities will be different, even characteristically different for whole populations, a great variety of arrangements ought to be expected and welcomed. Each of them will have its usefulness and its irritations; none of them will be permanent; the negotiation of difference will never produce a final settlement. What this also means is that our common humanity will never make us members of a single universal tribe. The crucial commonality of the human race is particularism: we participate, all of us, in thick cultures that are our own. With the end of imperial and totalitarian rule, we can at last recognize this commonality and begin the difficult negotiations it requires.

I

All selves are self-divided (internally differentiated) in three different ways. Two of these I have already discussed in the course of my effort to give a thick account of social life and moral culture. First, the self divides itself among its interests and its roles; it plays many parts (not only across a lifetime, as in Shakespeare's famous lines, but across a day or week) in relation to the different social goods available to it and the performances required of it in the different spheres of justice. The self is a citizen, parent, worker or professional or merchant, teacher or student, doctor or patient, and so on, defining itself in terms of its responsibilities, qualifications, skills, and entitlements. And, second, the self divides itself among its identities; it answers to many names, defining itself now in terms of its family, nation, religion, gender, political commitment, and so on. It identifies itself with different histories, traditions, rituals, holidays, and, above all, with different groups of other people, incorporated, as it were, into a wider selfhood.

I want to add now that, third, the self also divides itself among its ideals, principles, and values; it speaks with more than one moral voice—and that is why it is capable of self-criticism and prone to doubt, anguish, and uncertainty. Of course, this last division overlaps with the other two—the three cut across one another—making the self a wonderfully complex entity, which is matched to, which reflects and is reflected in, the complexity of the social world. But before I try to draw any large conclusions about this

85

two-way complexity or show how it supports the versions of pluralism I have defended in domestic and international society, I must look closely at the third division and the activity it makes possible. The self is the subject and object of self-criticism, our most anomalous and, perhaps, our most important moral enterprise. For the pluralism of roles and identities, and the practical possibility of complex equality and (collective) self-determination, depend on this internal reflection and debate. We need to think critically about the parts we play and the identities we affirm. But how can we do this when these same parts and identities are constitutive of the self that does the thinking?

II

To be oneself, according to the *Oxford English Dictionary*, is "to be in one's normal condition of body or mind" or, even better, to act in ways dictated by "one's true character, without hypocrisy or constraint." On the other hand, to be "outside" oneself (archaic) or "beside" oneself (contemporary) is to be deranged, "out of one's mind." But when I criticize myself, so it is usually said, I deliberately take a stand outside myself, detached, removed, looking on from a distance. I become the stern inspector of my "normal condition" or "true character," always found wanting. Working hard at self-criticism, am I out of my mind?

It isn't easy to say what I do when I criticize myself. Who is the "I" that does the criticizing? Who is the "self" that is criticized? What is it that I divide, who is in charge of the division, when I set one part of me to watch and judge the other(s)? What am I doing now, as I write these words and watch the watcher in myself? What roles, identities, and values make me or some part of me a critic? What other roles, identities, and values, what other parts of me, are the objects of criticism? And once I have mapped the lines of division, how do I know which are my better parts?

Social criticism, by contrast, is easier to describe. One member of society criticizes the others, or he criticizes the social arrangements for which the others are responsible. The difference between him (the critic) and them (the criticized) is clear. So is their relative moral standing, at least as seen by him. Whether the critic is a heroic figure or not, he at least exempts himself from the criticism he directs at the others. He is doing the best he can, and he isn't responsible, once he has spoken out, if the others refuse to listen. (I won't consider here whether his obligation extends beyond speaking out—to more difficult political acts like organizing, demonstrating, and so on. At some point, in any case, he is no longer responsible.) Self-criticism doesn't seem to offer a similar exemption. It would be odd to claim that since I am criticizing myself, I don't need to be criticized by anyone else. If my friends and neighbors crowd around, eager to join in, I can say to them, "Go away, don't criticize me, I'm doing it myself." But they may well feel that though this "I" is a good fellow, the "self" would probably benefit from a little extra castigation. Still, self-criticism is commonly thought an exemplary activity. We mostly approve of the self-critical self, even if we think the criticism richly deserved. And I approve too: I look at myself critically, and then I look approvingly at myself looking at myself critically. Perhaps my criticism deflates me; but then the spectacle of myself as critic puffs me up again.

If this is right, why is self-criticism so often painful? A certain amount of pain is necessary, I suppose, to justify the approval: if criticism didn't hurt, it wouldn't be exemplary. But self-criticism sometime produces what we might think of as surplus pain—not merely embarrassment, chagrin, regret, or remorse, but a paralyzing sense of inadequacy, endless guilt and self-loathing, which reach far beyond the requirements of the critical enterprise. We can all think of people for whom self-loathing would be entirely appropriate, but those are not the people likely to launch the enterprise in the first place. The average self probably "needs" only limited criticism, finite pain. But perhaps the enterprise, once launched, has a momentum of its own. The harder I look, the worse I appear. Social critics get tired, burned out, choked by their own anger, while self-critics simply improve with practice. Or perhaps the self-critic is taken unawares. Slowly he strips away his protective clothing, thinking all the while that what lies underneath isn't half bad, and then finds himself staring in horror at his own hideous nakedness. The pain comes from the surprise.

This last sounds like a Christian account: the critical "I," religiously identified, face-to-face with original sin, corrupted flesh, the fallen Adam. But the religious critic presumably knows what to expect; he has been forewarned. Surprise is easier to understand if we tell (the conventional version of) a Freudian story. For isn't "the instinctual strength of the id" always a painful surprise to the civilized superego? There doesn't seem any other way to explain the superego's judgmental fury as it punishes the ego for behavior (and for thoughts and wishes) to which it yields as to "necessities of nature."[56] So I am handed over to what claims to be my best part. The story doesn't end there, of course, for the pain of discovery and repression can be cured or at least ameliorated through psychoanalysis (though not without additional pain along the way). I am not sure exactly how the cure works, never having experienced it, but I suggest that we think of analysis as a kind of metacritique. It requires an extended criticism of the critical "I" and a partial vindication of the castigated self. The vindication can never be more than partial. The superego, even if we reject its most far-reaching claims, is still the internal representative of moral value (and of the

---

[56] Sigmund Freud, *Civilization and its Discontents*, trans. James Strachey (New York: W. W. Norton, 1962), pp. 72ff., 90.

demands of role and identity), and I cannot live in civilized society, I cannot live in the company of others, without its ministrations. The self requires its critic even if it then requires its analyst. The discontents of civilization are permanent. But insofar as I can generate and sustain (with the help of the analyst) a second critical "I," critical of the first, the discontent need not be paralyzing. This is Freud's great insight: the superego bears watching at least as much as any of my other parts.

If psychoanalysis explains the pain, philosophy explains the pride of self-criticism. In the psychoanalytic tradition, it is the instincts that are universal, while the critical standards by which the instincts are judged are always the standards of a particular culture. The id is the old Adam, and "in Adam's fall/we perished all." The superego, by contrast, is a human artifact, a social creation, different in different times and places, enforcing different rules and regulations, with different degrees of rigor and zeal. But these differences make only a marginal difference, for the function of the superego is determined not by its own particularist content but by the universal id, which is always there and always in need of repression. The philosophical view reverses the terms of this argument. Now it is the castigated self that is various in form and parochial in content, the product of this or that local history, while the critical "I" is in touch or at least aspires to be in touch with universal values. Self-criticism for the philosopher is much like social criticism (for the philosopher): it is a kind of reflection in tranquility, a scrutiny of the self *sub specie aeternitatis*. I step back, detach myself from my self, create a new moral agent, let's call him superagent, who looks at the old one, me, as if I were a total stranger.[57] Superagent

---

[57] On what it might mean to take an "objective" view of the world and of oneself as part of it, see Thomas Nagel, *The View from Nowhere* (New York: Oxford University Press, 1986).

studies me as one among the others, no different from the others, and applies to all of "them," including me, objective and universal moral principles.

Naturally, I am found wanting. Superagent is not found wanting: who could make the finding? I could of course step back again, detach myself again, create an ultra-agent, but what could ultra-agent say that superagent has not already said? Psychoanalysis makes things simpler: the analyst can criticize the superego because the superego embodies, if that is the right word, a merely particular morality. But the critical "I" imagined by the philosopher speaks for morality itself. It is the philosopher's alter ego projected into (though rarely assimilated or naturalized within) the particular self.

The aim of the analyst is to establish a new balance of power within the self, modifying the rule of civilized values, controlling (but not destroying) the lordly superego. The aim of the philosopher is to win the internal war, to make superagent supreme within the self. Consider, for example, Jean-Paul Sartre's account of the self-creation of the intellectual, "the guardian of fundamental ends," that is, of universal values.[58] The intellectual achieves his guardianship "by constantly criticizing and radicalizing [himself]." This self, says Sartre, speaking of his own case, is the product of "petty-bourgeois conditioning." It is, again, a merely particular self, legitimately subject therefore to the devastations of criticism. Insofar as the criticism is successful, one arrives at a historically and morally departicularized self—a superior being presumably. Sartre admits, indeed, that we never quite reach this happy condition (noncondition?): ours is "a divided consciousness, that can never be

---

[58] Jean-Paul Sartre, "A Plea for Intellectuals" in *Between Existentialism and Marxism*, trans. John Mathews (New York: Pantheon, 1975), pp. 259–263.

healed." We must, however, aim at healing; the end of division remains the ideal destination of the critical "I." But what if one thinks the self even more divided than Sartre acknowledges? And what if one admires the "divided consciousness?"

III

Taken as accounts of self-criticism, both the psychoanalytic and the philosophical models belong to the category of the "thin." They suggest a simple linear and hierarchical arrangement of the self, with a single critical "I" at the top of the line and a single line of criticism. (Think of this "I" as the virtuous citizen-self or the rational maximizing-self of my earlier account in Chapter Two.) Analysts want to modify the hierarchy, philosophers to vindicate it, but neither doubts its existence. The superego may represent only a particular understanding of value, but it represents value nonetheless; it is the internal agent of civilization, a secularized version of the religious conscience. The analyst is also a hierarchical superior, the external agent not only of civilization but also of mental health. The superiority of the philosopher's critical "I" is even more obvious, for it claims to speak in the name of "fundamental ends." No doubt these models capture something of our inner experience—the guilt we feel, for example, when we do something obviously wrong, when superego and superagent, blaming us, seem to speak for everyone in the world, without ambiguity or complexity. They are most plausible and persuasive when they represent our minimalist morality. But the two models also miss a great deal. They miss the common immediacy of selfhood when we live by what might be called our critical instincts, without the ministrations of any internal autocrat. And they miss those moments of doubt and division when it is radically unclear which part is our best part, which roles, identities, or values are fundamental. The hierarchical view requires a thick, pluralist, and democratic correction.[59]

I will begin with the defense of immediacy and then move quickly on, for the two are closely connected, to the critique of hierarchy. A couple of examples will help the argument along. In one of his brilliant and savage essays attacking America's involvement in World War I, Randolph Bourne contemplates and then rejects the designation of himself as a "conscientious objector." He doesn't, indeed, want to fight, but it's not the case that he "would be delighted to work up [his] blood lust for the business [of fighting], except that this unaccountable conscience, like a godly grandmother, absolutely forbids." What forbids his military service is "something that is woven into his whole modern philosophic feel for life."[60] Bourne claims that his refusal is the act of a *person*, not of an "objective conscience" suppressing the lower orders of the self. It is not his conscience that refuses but something deeper within, or more continually active across, or more pervasive throughout, his inner life. Perhaps this is a sign of ego strength or of a critical "I" already triumphant. I don't doubt that one could provide a psychoanalytic or philosophical account of Bourne's "feel for life." But there is no hierarchy without the lower orders, and they don't seem anywhere in evidence. Blood lust doesn't figure at all in Bourne's present state of mind; neither does it figure, as he tells the story, in any of his past states. He thinks and

---

[59] The same can be said of all the related hierarchies: reason/passion, mind/body, elite/mass, and so on. They are all similarly thin and in need of thickening—in need of some novel, but not crazy doctrine that blurs the lines, introduces new terms, challenges the standard attributions of value.

[60] Randolph Bourne, "Below the Battle" in *The World of Randolph Bourne*, ed. Lillian Schlissel (New York: E. P. Dutton, 1965), pp. 164–165.

acts in intimate accord with his feelings: the critical "I" has no place here.

Now consider a story in which it does have a place, but not a high or even an honorable one. In a well-known passage from the *Discourse on the Origin of Inequality*, Rousseau describes how the "tranquil sleep" of a philosopher is suddenly disturbed by cries for help. He hears the cries but cannot be torn from his bed.

> A murder may with impunity be committed under his window; he has only to put his hands in his ears and argue a little with himself to prevent nature, which is shocked within him, from identifying itself with the unfortunate sufferer. Uncivilized man has not this admirable talent; and for want of reason . . . is always foolishly ready to obey the first promptings of humanity.[61]

This nicely reverses the conventional hierarchy. The internalized voice of philosophy represses instinct and moral value at the same time. The critical "I" is watchful indeed, but this is a calculating and prudent watchfulness, wary of the traps of sentimental goodness. Is Rousseau endorsing the natural, precritical self? Not quite; he is too sophisticated for that. He doesn't believe that our internal wars have a single desirable outcome. He means to sow confusion about our better part.

In Rousseau's story, the philosopher's "first prompting" is to get out of bed, to help the person in need. But what he argues himself out of is not only this course of action but the sense of guilt that comes from not following it. The philosopher goes back to sleep contented with himself, and this is not a critical failure but, Rousseau tells us, a critical success. The internalized voice of philosophy is triumphant.

---

[61] Jean-Jacques Rousseau, *The Social Contract and Discourses*, trans. G. D. H. Cole (New York: E. P. Dutton, 1950), p. 226.

The conventional view of criticism and guilt is obviously very different. Self-criticism, on the conventional view, is the activity of prescribing guilt, and guilt is the prescribed feeling, dutifully accepted. Because I am or have been self-critical, I feel guilty. (Freud's argument is considerably more complicated, but the temporal order is, I think, the same.) This account, however, provides no emotional basis for the critical enterprise. Isn't it sometimes the case that I criticize myself because I already feel guilty? Self-criticism is an interested investigation into the reasons for the feeling— or, as Rousseau suggests, it is an attempt to repress the feeling. Most often, the critical "I" goes to work knowing that the self is bad or has acted badly. The verdict is in; the goal now is to figure out what lies behind it.

The conventional view is probably more logical: first the prosecuting attorney and the judge's verdict, then the (self-) punishment and the pain of guilt. But the alternative account is psychologically more plausible, for it captures something of the intimacy of the self with itself. Now the picture is more complex: I don't wait upon the indictment of a prosecuting attorney, for he has, as it were, assistants in my mind and heart—and I have intimations of moral understanding that precede his accusation. I am already in pain. There is no precritical self.

I do, of course, reflect in tranquility on things I have said and done. I read over my life, and sometimes I am a critical reader. How does this activity compare to the more immediate form of self-criticism? It is like rereading an essay or book that I wrote years ago. The passage of time makes for critical distance. I tell myself that someone else is the author of these pages, and so I read them with more objectivity than I could ever have managed when I was writing them. Yes, but with less interest. I am indeed disinterested and dispassionate, or relatively so, but perhaps interest and passion are crucial features of the self-critical enterprise. Contrast my criticism now and my worrying then (when I was writing). The first is more objective, the second more . . . critical. Worrying is a kind of running self-criticism, the work of a truly engaged critic (but not of a single-minded critic: I worry simultaneously about different things, often inconsistently). When I am writing, I probably worry too much about getting each sentence exactly right; later on I care too little about whether I actually got it right. Which is the privileged position? We miss the mark in different ways.

But there is a difference between criticizing the self and criticizing the products or the activities of the self. Actions, words, even whole books of words, can be taken back, repudiated, apologized for; but I can't so easily take back myself. I promise to change not merely what I do but what I am. This is, however, a promise rarely redeemed. Refashioning the person, like revolutionizing society, is likely to turn out to be a very incomplete achievement. No doubt, the critical voice that tells me that it's not what I have done that's bad, it's me, cuts very deep. But I can take comfort in the fact that this critic is also me—some part of me turned upon the rest, demanding to be vindicated, not transformed. And I can always ask for a second opinion from another part of me, and for a third. The critics to whom I turn for these additional opinions don't stand at different temporal distances from my self; now distance is best imagined spatially. I have different values, alternative ego ideals or conceptions of what I ought (or want) to be like, which exist, as it were, at different removes from what I actually am. I have, let's say, fantasies of saintliness, but the critical voice that speaks for saintliness doesn't speak with much immediacy or passion. This self-critic is relatively distant and disinterested since it knows (I know) that I am never going to hit that mark. But I would also like to be more compassionate, more sensitive to the needs of others, more articulate in engaging them and drawing them out—and here every criticism of failed attempts or non-attempts causes pain. This self-critic speaks from closer up.

My inner world is thickly settled. Remember again Yeats's line about how we have to choose "perfection of the life, or of the work." It's no use pretending that the same critical "I," in touch with universal and objective value, defends these opposed perfections. I am in fact assaulted by different critics making different claims on behalf of different and often inconsistent notions of a more perfect self. Indeed, I am assaulted by critics who defend what I might otherwise take to be imperfection, for sometimes (when I imagine myself in the marketplace, say) I would like to be more calculating, more aggressive, more systematically focused on my own career than I commonly am. And that too is self-criticism. Perhaps I should picture my self-critics as critics not only of me but of one another. I am an object of attack and also an observer of the critical wars.

I am not, nor is any one of my self-critics, the sovereign director of these critical wars. The critics that crowd around, speaking for different values, representing different roles and identities, have not been chosen by me. *They are me*, but this "me" is socially as well as personally constructed; it is a complex, maximalist whole. I am urged to conduct myself, let's say, as a good citizen, doctor, or craftsman; or I am condemned for not conducting myself as a faithful American, Jew, black, woman, or whatever. Many external "causes" are represented in my critical wars, and the representatives come from and still have connections outside. They have been internalized, in the common phrase, and, if I am lucky, naturalized—adapted to their new environment (my mind and heart) and to the requirements of competitive co-existence. None of them aspires, if I am lucky, to the part of superego or superagent, aiming at singular and absolute domination.

The surplus pain of self-criticism is probably the effect of domination. This is one of the pathologies of the self—as is its anarchic opposite, when the critical wars are fought without restraint, and I am literally torn apart by my crit-

ics, unable to make even short-term choices among them:
distraught and anxious. But continual skirmishing is part
of a normal life, and so is the (negotiated) truce, when we
experience what Bourne described: the immediacy of a self
at peace with its critics, knowing what it has to do.

Can I say that I am challenged and corrected by more
than one conscience? (Can Socrates be imagined with
more than one daimon?) "Consciences" is an odd plural
when applied to a single self. In *Paradise Lost*, Milton's God
claims to have placed within each of us "My Umpire Conscience."[62] One God, one umpire: singularity is transitive.
A secular view suggests a more complicated placement.
Conscience means shared (moral) knowledge, and if we
share this knowledge with other people rather than with
God, we will also share divergent accounts and interpretations of its meaning. So conscience is itself divided. My
home-plate umpire calls a strike but is overruled by my
third-base umpire. Mostly, I relish these internal disagreements (much as I relish political conflicts); sometimes, they
are very hard to live with. Perhaps this difficulty accounts
for my acceptance, sometimes, of a thinner conception of
the self, according to which God's singular umpire, or
someone else's, rules supreme.

Here again, the comparison with social criticism is
useful. Surely society is served best if its critics number
more than one. Not a single critic, standing in a privileged
place, upholding a uniform and universal standard, but
a variety of critics with competing standards: then, assuming that there is an agent (a democratic public, say)
capable of choosing among its critics—even though it
can't choose the critics themselves—there is also room for
choice. There are alternative claims and proposals to
which we have to listen, which can't be silenced by some

---

[62] John Milton, *Paradise Lost* III: 195.

all-powerful, once-and-for-all, ideologically correct argument. The case is the same with self-criticism. I am served
best if I have many internal critics. Pluralism makes for
freedom because it leaves room for the canniness of the
self. But there does have to be a self capable of canniness,
strong enough to absorb all the criticisms directed against
it and to judge among them.

The self is indeed divided, but it isn't (except in patho-
logical cases) utterly fragmented. I can be strong and
consistent in this role or identity and then in that one; I
can act on behalf of this value and then that one—much
as a democratic state, despite fierce and on-going political
controversy, can pursue a particular set of policies and then
a different set. Without a coherent public, social criticism
loses its point; without a coherent self, an ego, a *me*, the
point of self-criticism is similarly lost.[63] The picture of the
self that I want to defend is *ordered*, even if the order is
also, as we will see, always subject to change. I can think
of myself as a confabulation of critics only if I am some-
how at the center of the confabulation: not quite in charge
of all the critics but their only listener and answerer, ready
to say yes or no (or maybe) to each of them.

IV

There is no linearity, then, and no hierarchy. The order
of the self is better imagined as a thickly populated circle,
with me in the center surrounded by my self-critics who
stand at different temporal and spatial removes (but don't
necessarily stand still). Insofar as I am receptive to criti-

---

[63] See the discussion of the self as the subject to which action is "im-
puted" in Paul Ricoeur, *Oneself as Another,* trans. Kathleen Blamey
(Chicago: University of Chicago Press, 1992), pp. 292–293.

cism, ready for (a little) castigation, I try to draw some of the critics closer, so that I am more immediately aware of their criticism; or I simply incorporate them, so that they become my intimate worriers, and I become a worried self. I am like a newly elected president, summoning advisors, forming a cabinet. Though he is called commander-in-chief, his choices in fact are limited, his freedom qualified; the political world is full of givens; it has a history that predates his electoral triumph. My inner world is full of givens, too, culturally bestowed or socially imposed—I maneuver among them insofar as their plurality allows for the maneuvering. My larger self, my worried self, is constituted and self-constituted by the sum of them all. I am the whole circle and also its embattled center.

This at least is the thick view of the self. But what are we to make of an individual whose every word and act invite a thin description? Consider what I will call the dominated self, who identifies whole-heartedly with, or yields everything to, a single all-powerful critic. The religious or political fanatic is the obvious example: god-possessed or ideologically driven. He is always angry or worried about the same thing, though he often succeeds in projecting these feelings onto the external world. The self is overwhelmed by the critical "I," which is itself immune from criticism. The ultra-nationalist is a self of a similar sort, I think, and so is the person who chooses Yeats's "perfection of the work," judging every human relationship, valuing every social good, in terms of its contribution to his singular pursuit of power or wealth . . . or truth or beauty. All these cases represent the end of Sartre's "divided consciousness," and though this is an end that Sartre claimed to find desirable, it seems to me very unattractive. For it can't be the case that the all-powerful critical "I" stands alone. We must imagine it dominating other self-critics, repressing alternative possibilities within the self. No one growing up in the modern world is, as it were, linear before the fact. Only repression will make us

so. I am not going to try to describe here the psychologi-
cal mechanisms of repression (I argued in the fourth
chapter for the role of fear in shaping a singular national
identity). I only want to insist that such mechanisms must
be at work in every person whose "true character" or "normal condition" is singular and absolute. Within every thin
self, there is a thick self yearning for elaboration, largeness,
freedom.

The fanatic, the ideologue, the "ultra," the perfection-
ist who cares about nothing but his own work: all these
people are *not listening*, deaf not only to outside voices
(like yours and mine) but also to inside voices. The critics
are always there, embodying or speaking for the possibilities of the culture and the larger self. But if every one of
these critics has a position—not merely a place in the
geography of the mind but also a doctrine and an argument—what is the position of the self-that-is-criticized? Is
the center a zone of neutrality? Does it have a content? If
it does, it must be a changing content, for the self as I have
described it, the listening self, absorbs criticism, incor-
porates critics: it isn't in time present what it was in time
past. I am constituted in part by my self-critics. But I must
also be imagined—so I have argued—as an agent capable
of maneuvering among my constituent parts. Obviously, I
imagine myself that way, and my self-critics agree, if only
in order to condemn my maneuvers. For them, as for me,
the "subject" is alive and well, though always under pressure. In similar fashion, a democratic public changes its
character without losing its collective identity or sense of
agency, as it listens and responds to social criticism.

But what is it that governs the response? Is it the sheer
persuasiveness of the critics? Are different societies and
different selves susceptible to different sorts of criticism?
Are there some (minimal) structural prerequisites of
society and selfhood to which even the most severe (maximalist) critics must adjust? I don't know the answers to
these questions. At its center, the self is what it is, "perdur-

able," as Lionel Trilling liked to say, though its configura-
tion changes over the course of its endurance.[64] It is, of
course, a historical and social product; so, more obviously,
is each internal critic of the self, reflecting the values of its
time and place. But the production and reproduction of
selves, and even of self-critics, is a great mystery. Every self
is its own self, different from all the others, in need of its
own critical circle, responsive and resistant in its own
ways. (Every society is its own society, different from all
the others, in need of its own critical circle, and so on.)
There is no ideal pattern of internal relations.

I am inclined to say, of course, that thick, divided selves
are the characteristic products of, and in turn require, a
thick, differentiated, and pluralist society. It does not follow
from this assertion, however, that there is a single ideal
thickness of the self that can only be matched by one kind
of accommodating society or that there is a single ideal
thick society that can only be matched by one kind of
adaptable self. No doubt, we can give thin accounts of
accommodation and adaptability, and sometimes it is politically useful to do that, arguing for a social or personal
version of a minimalist liberalism. But such arguments will
only take us so far; they can't reach to the reality of our
private or our collective lives.

The reality is this: specific sets of thick selves find themselves more or less at home in specific complex societies.
There are always mismatches, but we can try to draw the
(internal and external) boundaries of the society in such
a way as to reduce the pain they cause. The boundaries are
drawn politically, and we might usefully imagine not only

---

[64] Lionel Trilling, *Sincerity and Authenticity* (Cambridge, Mass.: Har-
vard University Press, 1972), p. 99. See the discussion in Mark
Krupnick, *Lionel Trilling and The Fate of Cultural Criticism* (Evanston,
Ill.: Northwestern University Press, 1986), esp. chapter 9.

individual citizens but all the self-critics and criticized selves out of which these citizens are constituted as participants in this politics. Consider, for example, one powerful contemporary self-critic who defends (in my inner debates and probably in yours) the modern ego-ideal of a healthy, lean, and unaddicted self. This critic is challenged, let's say, by the internal voice of skepticism and irony, and even more strongly by the voice of desire, but it makes sufficient headway, has sufficient effects on both attitudes and conduct, so as to become a factor in our political arguments about justice. It no longer seems right to think of addictive drugs, including cigarettes and alcohol, simply as marketable commodities. Mandatory health warnings, restrictions on advertising, bans on smoking in public spaces, and a variety of other measures redraw the boundaries of the market and the understanding of property and privacy rights. If in my own case skepticism and desire have (temporarily) won out, then I am mismatched among and probably overmatched by all the healthy, lean, and unaddicted others. Still, in a society of divided selves and separated spheres, I am likely to find comrades enough and space enough to survive—peaked, paunchy, and addicted. And that too is a matter of justice.

The case is the same with questions of role and identity. My many-sided self (assailed from all sides) requires a thickly differentiated society in which to express my different capacities and talents, my different senses of who I am. But if I am Don Quixote, lance in hand, tilting at windmills, I will be mismatched and overmatched. The available range of roles and identities in twentieth-century America doesn't extend to knighthood—and need not be extended. Any given society can only respond to a limited number of divided selves, and these are likely to be characteristically divided selves, listening or refusing to listen to roughly the same set of moral critics and self-critics, the products of a common history, speaking in a similar idiom. (That is why an internalist social criticism can generate indignation and guilt.) Societies have a particu-

lar, and a rightly particular, shape because their members
have characteristic selves. But because these selves are divided and their societies highly differentiated, points of
access should always exist for deviant members. Don
Quixote's experience will be relatively rare, though it can
never be avoided entirely.[65] In the sphere of recognition,
especially, some people will fare badly because of historical or cultural mismatches. We must protect their rights
in other spheres as best we can.

Divided selves are best accommodated by complex
equality in domestic society and by different versions of
self-determination in domestic and international society.
Different versions: not only the nation-state, which is most
obviously appropriate in those cases where a particular
identity is, as it were, under siege. Whenever the inner
voice that tells me I am a Jew, Armenian, Kurd, and so on,
finds only a problematic and dangerous external expression, the protective shelter that sovereignty alone provides
in the modern world seems morally appropriate, perhaps
even necessary. But I listen to other voices and so require
other forms of protection: religious toleration, cultural
autonomy, individual rights. It is not possible to pick out
the best protection, for no voice is necessarily or rightly
dominant; none of my self-critics has the last word. I am
not finally this or that—a finished self to whom we can fit
a finished set of social arrangements. Nor when I work on
myself, responding to criticism, struggling to fashion a
better self, do I work in accordance with a single or final
blueprint.

But now one of my self-critics looks askance at this plu-
ralizing argument and argues in turn that it is self-serving

---

[65] Nor would we want it avoided: the mismatched self, whose self-critics
come, as it were, from outside the familiar social world, presses against
the limits of our collective understandings and, sometimes, explores
the land beyond.

on my part. This democracy of criticism saves me from the harshness and persistence of a single supercritic. So I evade the voice of truth, waiting to tell me how bad I really am. Perhaps I am doing that; I can't say that I am incapable of such a strategy. I'm not, in fact, out of my mind. Even in my normal condition, however, I hear voices, I play parts, I identify myself in different ways—and so I must aim at a society that makes room for this divided self.

Acknowledgments

These five chapters were first brought together in their present form as the Frank M. Covey, Jr., Lectures in Political Analysis at Loyola University, Chicago, in 1993. I am grateful to Thomas Engeman who was the organizer, host, and resident critic for my visit to Loyola.

"Moral Minimalism" was originally a paper prepared for a conference sponsored by the Italian Library in Locarno, Switzerland, and organized by the Library's director Antonio Spadafora. The paper was published in *From the Twilight of Probability: Ethics and Politics*, ed. William Shea and Antonio Spadafora (Canton, Mass.: Science History Publications, USA, 1992). "Justice and Tribalism" is a revised version of an article published in *Dissent* in 1992 under the title "The New Tribalism." "The Divided Self" derives from a shorter piece that appeared in *Social Research* in 1987 as "Notes on Self-Criticism." The first four of these chapters were the basis of a set of lectures delivered at the Collège International de Philosophie in Paris in 1992. Chantal Mouffe set up those lectures for me and discussed them with me during my week in Paris.

In addition to the reviewers and commentators mentioned in the footnotes to these pages, there are others whose helpful, if sometimes sharp, criticism I want to acknowledge here: Joseph Carens, Joshua Cohen, Amy Gutmann, William Kymlicka, David Miller, Susan Okin, Joseph Raz, Nancy Rosenblum, Michael Rustin, Thomas Scanlon, Judith Shklar, Ian Shapiro, and Georgia Warnke. Unknowingly, all of them looked over my shoulder as I wrote and rewrote this book.

I am, as always, glad of the advice and assistance of colleagues, visiting members, and staff at the Institute for Advanced Study.

Index of Names